Dating Myself Unmasked

A Guiding Light from Sexual Trauma to Self-Acceptance

Dr. Danita Morales Ramos, PhD

Dating Myself Unmasked:
A Guiding Light from Sexual Trauma to Self-Acceptance

All Rights Reserved

Copyright © 2020 Danita Morales Ramos, PhD

This book may not be reproduced, transmitted, or stored in whole or part by any means, including graphic, electronic, or mechanical without the express written consent of the publisher except in the case of brief quotations embodied in critical articles and reviews.

ISBN: 978-1-63760-293-5

Imprint: Independently published

Cover design by BetiBup33 design studio

Dedication

To my daughter, Ascha, one of my heroes, who gave me the courage to be who I am without fear, and to all the women and men living in fear of being known.

The persona, which the individual's system of adaptation to, or manner he assumes in dealing with, the world. Every calling or profession, for example, has its own characteristic persona. It is easy to study these things nowadays when photographs of public personalities so frequently appear in the press. A certain kind of behaviour is forced on them by the world, and professional people endeavor to come up to these expectations. Only, the danger is that they become identical with their personas—the professor with his text-book, the tenor with his voice. The damage is done; henceforth he lives exclusively against the background of his own biography... One could say, with little exaggeration, that the persona is that which in reality one is not, but which oneself as well as others think one is.

C.G. Jung

(*The Archetypes and the Collective Unconscious*, pp. 122-123)

Table of Contents

Dedication i
Foreword ii
Preface iv
1. Introduction 4
2. Playing Victim (Abandoned Child) 9
3. Partnering Down (The Illusion of Rescue) 17
4. Becoming Prey (Neediness) 28
5. Wanting Closure (Low Self-Worth) 38
6. Hypersexuality (Infatuation) 42
7. Self-abandonment (Defense Mechanism) 46
8. Healing (Restoration of Self) 51
9. Forgiveness (Blame No One) 59
10. Self-acceptance (Celebrate Your Flaws) 69
11. Date Yourself First (Embrace Self-Worth) 77
12. A Roadmap for Dating (Accept Applications) 83
13. Build and Grow a Healthy Relationship (Commit) 116
14. Never Stop Dating You (Be Unmasked) 132
Follow with Dr. D 135
Acknowledgements 136
About the Author 137

Foreword

A mastermind group, the Lions Den, brought Danita and I together. I noticed the value she was providing the group and I had to connect with her. Since then, over two years have passed, and there are not many days where the two of us do not communicate. Shockingly, our two souls have never met in person, but our phones keep us deeply rooted. One day, in the very near future, I will convince her to journey up to the arctics of Wisconsin. I am honored to call her my friend, my 'hoop sister' and a source of energy that many cannot compare to.

Danita carries many names, labels and titles, but my favorite title she wears is the one I gave her—The Queen of Boundaries. I do not say that lightly, she is truly the Queen. Boundary here, you get a boundary, they get a boundary, boundaries for everyone. Do you know how one becomes the Queen of setting boundaries? TRUTH and going through a lot of shit and making it to the other side.

Another superpower she has is the ability to make you dig into the depths of your soul to find the deep, dark, and ugly truth you have been hiding. She protects that truth as if it were her own and makes you walk with that truth until it turns into power. There is so much light buried within our truth and all she wants to do is brighten up a room with that light.

Danita is real, she is human, she trips and falls just like the rest of us. But when she falls, she gets right back up, swears a little and continues to move forward. She is unstoppable, fearless, and powerful.

Truth is the only thing printed on these pages. There is truth in her tears, in her words and in her life. As you read her words, let her truth seep into your fingertips, up your arm, over your shoulder and let that truth hit your heart. I promise your world will become a little less dark.

I read her first book and I loved it, but I told her I wanted more. Thank you for giving us more.

Your Forever Friend,

Rachel Pader

Preface

I thought I was something that I am not. I am about to share with you my journal about the mental surgery that I conducted to remove another cancer in my psyche—self-hate. My memoir, *From the Voice of a Fractured Mind: Speak Loud*, was the start of my exploration of self. In it, I conceptualized six self-defeating beliefs that contribute to mental health problems in individuals, to include me, such as depression, anxiety, and suicidality. Here in *Dating Myself UNMASKED*, I go deeper to uncover engrained consciousnesses and personalities. I expose, without apology, details of my past trauma and the secrets that I have kept from others, but more troubling, from myself.

I wrote this book modeling the way that I provide therapy educating on relatable truths and providing clarity on trauma and give practical strategies on how to engage with those truths. Engaging in healthy ways with these truths has helped me to improve my mental, physical, and relational quality of life. I believe they can do the same for you. In the first part of the book, I journaled my purest recollection of past trauma and hurts sharing my reaction to the same. Trauma work can be triggering and uncomfortable. Isolation, relationship conflict, mood disorders, suicidality, and self-hate that resulted from past trauma have been the biggest contributor for clients to seek my therapeutic services. I recommend seeking a qualified trauma therapist, in conjunction with reading this book, if you have any history of trauma. In the second part of the book, I impart practical concepts and tools I created to assist my clients and overcome my own self-hate that nearly robbed me of experiencing the love of my life—the love of self.

As a clinical psychologist and expert in the areas of self-concealment, perceived discrimination, and major depression, I know that personas or wearing masks contribute significantly to mental sickness. I conducted research on self-concealment, perceived discrimination, and major depression building on existing literature about self-disclosure in my doctoral research. My findings support my belief that self-disclosure rather than self-concealment is the antidote for depression and other mood disorders—as given people's tendency to hide who they truly are produces significant clinical emotional distress. At least that has been the case for most of the thousands of patients I have treated, except for those with a severe psychosis. Self-disclosure, the act of exposing one's true self, in my opinion, is an attitude toward life that combats self-disturbance such as negative self-talk (DE-pressed talk), attempting to predict the future (anxiety), and paranoia (distrust). Exposing one's true self leads to psychological and emotional liberation, which can in turn improve interpersonal relations with family, friends, coworkers, and partners. Living a life exposed is the art of being a human. Just as the dog goes through life being a dog—never trying to be a cat or a rabbit or some other animal—so should the human travel his lifetime as himself, not living a charade, without fear of judgment from self or others.

I. Introduction

Here I go again.

I am laughing inside as I write this book. I thought that in my first book, *From the Voice of a Fractured of Mind: Speak Loud*, I had unleashed all of me—the true me. I believed that in it I revealed all my secrets, tools, and epiphanies and felt there was nothing left for me to share. I was in denial.

Addicts often live in denial, though I could not deny my inability to speak. The voice that boldly spoke and advocated for others was silent to self once again. In the midst of the 2020 pandemic--also called the *scamdemic* or *plandemic*--noise, I could hear something in my silence, although I wasn't sure what I was hearing. The silence became unbearable. I had become comfortable, and by comfortable, I mean that I allowed myself to focus on what was easy. It was easy to focus on what was going on outside of me like the overly propagated health crisis. It allowed me to ignore the mental health crisis going on inside of me. My ignorance thickened my silence.

Normally, the silence overwhelms, so I make more noise. This time, the silence was leading me through another phase in my spiritual journey. The senseless quarantines and lockdowns pushed me toward needing and wanting to expose more. In March 2020, I felt angry and defenseless against a conforming American society and world that made me start writing again. I hate conformity. Some non-elite American citizens conformed by policing those who did not conform to social distancing. Some closed their businesses. Meanwhile, the elite government watched its citizens rage in civil war. I became a spectator and skeptic watching as face masks were mandated accessories exposing the comatose masses of conformity. With their printed masked expressions, some with clown faces and others adorned with rhinestones, the world became enslaved not by a physical virus but the collaborative compliance to be silenced. Their masked silence demonstrated their perceived lack of power or what they called "The New Normal."

I refused to call it that as I watched firsthand therapy session after therapy session that the masking caused a psychological sickening more accurately described as "The New Abnormal." In my silence, I became awakened. Though I rebelled most of the year by not wearing a mask or cloth covering, I secretly had morphed into a muzzled isolation, which I began to see projected in the covered faces of my society. I rejected the "Be smart. Do Your Part...Stay 6 Feet Apart" because humans weren't meant to live in isolation. I declared once more to be something **to** the world (a voice) and not something **for** it (a slave). It meant running like a wild animal in a zoo shouting to all those caged in "Freedom!" Each therapy session I held showed me the fear of being exposed inside of individuals. These individuals had allowed an overreported health crisis, civil unrest, and political agendas to exacerbate other deep-seated issues such as low self-worth, conflicted sexuality, addiction, trauma, and emotional dysregulation. Most importantly, all seemed plagued with the inability to just BE.

To BE?

I, too, struggled with *being* yet sitting in silence made pause. Erling Kagge, in his *Silence: In the Age of Noise,* described silence or the pause as unbusying one's self from technology and reclaiming freedom. That is, unplugging from Facebook, Instagram, Twitter, Tik Tok, and the others, which I conceptualize as a real-world *Matrix*. As I paused, I uncovered trauma that still was buried within me—a psychic phenomenon.

The covered faces I saw everywhere triggered wounds I thought were healed and some I did not realize existed. Chakra healing guided me out of the silence as I unblocked my third eye, throat, and heart chakras. These blockages had caused emotional poison and disease—silence, isolation, anxiety, chronic pain, sexual tension, apathy, and depression—that could only be cured through a spiritual awakening. Silence, the most intense of these ailments, represented another persona or personality, as Jung would call it. I realized that I had multiple personalities, as it were. I saw that my patients did too. Motivated by the desire to break the silence and speak for myself, I decided not only to break my silence but to promote others to break theirs, too. Hence, I resolved that for the sake of making it through 2020 and the rest of my life to date myself UNMASKED.

Part I: Unmasking the Personas

Trauma is a fact of life. It does not, however, have to be a life sentence.

~Peter A. Levine~

2. Playing Victim (Abandoned Child)

With the break in the silence, I began unmasking from my very beginning--not quite from my day of birth by not too far away from it. I am evolving into a beautiful human being and god who is full of life. Through my 2020 evolution, I started writing and got writer's block after three chapters. The words stopped flowing because I was writing lies, trying to uphold some perceived standard. I felt I needed to be scholarly since I was a published author already. It was not as authentic or assertive as I encourage the clients I see at my private practice, Azz-ert Urself! LLC Mindset Coaching & Counseling. I referred to the phenomenon of acting for others as "people-pleasing" in my first book. The chapters sounded like some boring professor hiding behind her PhD.

As I drove through the beautiful mountains of Harrisonburg, Pennsylvania, in mid-October 2020, I could hear my voice loud and clear. I heard something I had not heard in months, and it was something I needed to share with the world. I tried to take notes on my phone and on the back of business cards while driving as the ideas rushed to my head. The voice said "Write your personal dating journey. Journal dating yourself." I thought to myself, or rather I heard myself asking, "Would I date me? Why would I or why not?" I questioned myself more intently, "Do I really know me or am I running a scam of my own?" The more I asked, the clearer my vision became for this book. Along with it came new clarity on what ailed me, and I saw myself creating another work of art unfiltered and untamed.

A work of art starts with a vision in the mind of the artist, who then crafts it onto her canvas for the world to engage with. I have not always seen myself as a work of art, and my view of my past had a lot to do with that. But I know God is continuing to craft me into his vision of wholesomeness. This journal will take you through that past deeply, not as before with little shocking details for small table talk. Rather, it will expose what I had hidden—what many people hide because they fear that they are too much different from the regular herd of humans. They fear physical and emotional death, which is why they masquerade around in conformity. If you are reading or listening to this, yes you, that ends today. We must come out of hiding. When we hide, we play the victim abandoning who we really are. We are human gods of light with the right to discover, inhabit, and illuminate the world as we see fit in our finite time, respecting one another's journeys on this rock.

In my finite discovery of self, I acknowledge I had felt abandoned as a child. I did some deep trauma work with a client, who I will call Jane, a few years prior to this writing that revealed she had felt abandoned by her parents. Jane gained insight into why she found it difficult to set boundaries with her parents, particularly her mother. From childhood through adulthood, she disclosed how her parents relied on her to make adult decisions for them and neglected their responsibility to parent her. She had difficult verbalizing the exact feeling of how she felt toward her parents. She reported that their conflict had carried over from childhood to adulthood. Jane longed for them to raise and nurture her. Using my gift of helping others gain mental clarity, it became clear to me the nature of the conflict. I said to Jane in one intense moment, "You felt abandoned." She looked amazed yet relieved at my epiphany. It was during her magical epiphany I had an epiphany of my own. I, too, felt abandoned. I lacked insight into this fact until that very moment. I also was clueless about how this feeling unconsciously motivated my entire life. I had assumed, prior to that, abandonment only related to physical desertion such as giving someone up for adoption or leaving someone on the street. I learned in that moment--which spun in my head for days afterward--that there is an emotional abandonment. A surge of memories and thoughts about my childhood flooded through my mind as I simultaneously was helping her to work through *her* abandonment.

My childhood went south when I was 5 or 6 years old and my parents divorced. It was a period that abruptly ended me seeing my dad in his garden or playing with Patches, our Dalmatian, in the backyard. It meant no more riding on the back of my daddy's bike as the proud little show off that I was. It was the end of living with both of my parents in the same house. Daddy's girl was forced to become a latchkey kid along with my brother as my mom worked long hours at multiple jobs to provide for us. Underdeveloped--mentally, emotionally, and physically--I became my brother and I's caregiver. This period also meant living between extended family members' homes and a project apartment initially.

The new living arrangements were drastically different from our privileged lifestyle and Deep Creek home, where dad I went crabbing a lot. The privileged lifestyle had enabled me to be babysat by a Christian family neighbor, whose beliefs and practices aligned with what my parents modeled before their separation from each other. Our new arrangement left me inadequately supervised frequently by a friend of my mother—a project mother with lupus and her unsupervised children. Though she was my mother's friend, she was ill-equipped to care for me or my brother. I felt tossed like the wind and waves as I was left with her and relatives.

Being tossed about turned out to be more than just logistically spending time at different homes. It was a tumultuous time that included a series of unfortunate events. I'm not blaming my parents. They gave me the best they had to offer. They gave me life and love in the way that they understood it then and with the resources they had. They provided shelter, food, love, and life skills that I still hold to this day. I did not turn out half bad—as they say. But, as a child with an underdeveloped sense of what it takes to live in this world and raise a family, I misinterpreted their provision and the uncertainty of my whereabouts as abandonment. I looked at the world and people utterly confused and not having a name or label nor explanation to apply to what I was experiencing as a child. I buried the uncertainty and showed the world many created personalities—not all of them good.

There were two unfortunate events that happened early in my development that influenced these personas. I am uncertain the exact age, possibly 7 or 8, but it was before I was 9 years old. One experience involved me and two other girls, and the other experience involved a girl, a boy, and me. I am certain that the latter resulted in what was called in the black community "an ass whooping" after being caught in the act at a relative's house. I am certain that the former incident occurred at the babysitter's home while she was downstairs. The incident involved one of her girls saying, "Shhh, don't tell anyone" when she heard someone walking up the stairs. I was scared to share my feelings about the first incident especially after my beating. I also was ashamed to tell the first incident to my parents or anyone because I really did not know what the incident meant. Though, I did believe it was disgusting. This incidences I believed were out of my control or forced on me as I was too young to know what I was consenting to.

When you are forced to sit "quarantined" and isolated with your thoughts due to a war over the presidential office during a pandemic, you start to think and question everything-even your existence, choices, mortality, and *your* past. The thoughts of past incidences were troubling to say the least. As a clinical psychologist who specializes in treating trauma, I recognize that my intrusive thoughts triggered repressed memories about those past events, sex itself, and my own sexuality. I can share story after story about my exposure to confusing sexual experiences through childhood and some of my adulthood. The problem I faced, similar with many trauma survivors, is the earlier the trauma, the more intertwined the negative effects of that trauma is in the psyche. I questioned my sexuality most of my life and did not feel safe sharing it with anyone. My lack of sharing related to the fear of being harshly judged as a Christian, a woman with melanin skin, and being labeled as lesbian, gay or bisexual. *I felt others labeling me was unfair when I wasn't sure what I labeled myself or if I accepted the notion that I should be labeled in the first place.* Like I said, I do not like conformity.

If there is any label, I will give my former self or persona, it is the label of victim. Feeling abandoned, whether consciously or unconsciously, enabled me to play the victim even when I could have taken control of my life. Playing the victim, I overshared memories of trauma with unhealthy partners that emotionally exposed me. I was often rejected, abused, and controlled in these relationships resulting in substantial internal conflict. When I felt conflicted, it unconsciously motivated me more to deny myself. The unconscious denial was an irrational belief that I kept others from denying or abandoning me. I allowed some of my partners to either mentally, physically, or financially enslave me. Others I would chase even thought I knew they were emotionally unavailable. In any case, my abandonment was inevitable, yet I played the victim, religiously hoping it was not. In my vicious cycle of toxicity and victimhood, I developed more personas--detached, depressed, anxious, and aggressive--masked under the victim persona.

The victim persona looked for love in all the wrong places--liquor bottles, beer cans, marijuana, one-night stands, affairs, cyber dating (back in the '90s before it was the thing) and controlling friendships and partner relationships. I was bat crazy trying to make mental sense out of my mental chaos. Even when it became too overwhelming, I stayed in the feedback loop—victim, addict, victimizer, addict, and victim again.

3. Partnering Down (The Illusion of Rescue)

Playing the victim included being victimized and victimizing while perceiving I was protecting myself. It seems somewhat understandable considering I was sexually traumatized in my elementary school years. (Parents: That is why it is never too early to talk to your children about sex, sexuality, and appropriate touching). What was challenging for me was determining if I was protecting myself from boys or girls after my initial sexual traumas. Growing up, my mom and dad could not be around all the time. My mom never worked less than three jobs, and my dad worked 12 hours minimum in another city. Being raised in a strict Christian home, I had no clue how to tell my parents about the sexual event I experienced at the sitter's house. Two things I was sure of at that age if I did tell. I was destined for the fate of Sodom and Gomorrah if I told my parents about those girls or if I told them about my cousins and I had "played house." So, telling was out of the question. I tried not to think about it either because I didn't even want the all-knowing God to know. I buried those thoughts of abomination into my mind and believed all who shared in these experiences had done so as well.

I felt the sitter's two little girls, for example, had buried what I convinced myself was unforgiveable. My mother and I ran into them in the mall one day. At time, the girls and I were high schoolers. We had all physically grown up since that day in the small project apartment. Sadly, their mother had died years earlier from lupus. I stared at them wondering as my mother spoke with their caretaker how they seemed so "normal" when what we had done was to me "abnormal." Much like everyone walking around in 2020 who acted as if what was happening that year was *normal*, the girls innocently smiled masking just as they had done years before when that person walked up stairs startling them from their indiscretions. I thought to myself "You sneaky little bitches," feeling that they were shushing me again. I never saw them again, but I secretly hated both of them, surmising that they somehow changed my view of sexuality and of myself.

I would be lying if I said these girls were the only girls I encountered. After my experience with those two girls, I had infrequent relations with another girl close to my age. Again, lack of supervision as well as what I assume may have been curiosity had this girl and I acting out sexually toward one another. We never talked about it. It just always happened. We "knew" to go back to normal whenever someone was around. As we grew up together, we shared many stories about our boyfriends and lovers, but we never talked about what had gone on for years between us. One day she asked me while we were alone doing what we had done for many years, "Why do you always do that?" I was bewildered, and I asked, "Do what?" She said, "That!" I stopped "that" immediately once she said it but sat there asking myself the same question. I felt ashamed, as it was in *that* moment I realized from elementary school into my early twenties, I had done "that" with her, and she had done "that" with me. We had never asked each other if it was okay for "that" or if we even wanted "that." My shame came because I couldn't even remember how "that" started between us. I laid there while she tried to apologize because I became distant, only remembering the sneaky little bitches who had done "that" to me.

There was a pattern that had I developed over those years of seeking "that" or accepting "that" when I became disconnected from men as that disconnection left me sexually frustrated. For example, I found myself one day back in the late '90s on the internet searching for a man for companionship and sex. Oddly, an older married woman solicited me while I surfed.

I initially thought it was a hilarious game of some sort. The game kept me on the internet late at night connecting with her, curious about her interest. I could never envision a life with her--or any woman for that matter. By life, I am referring to cohabitation or defining ourselves as a couple. This is what confused me. Why was I seeking out or opening up myself for these connections if I had no intention of it turning into something long-term. My deepest desire was a committed relationship with a strong, loving man and an unabandoned family. Then, "why," I asked myself, was I drawn to these infrequent secret encounters? This dilemma perplexed me.

My frustration about the dilemma with women frustrated me more at times than other sexual trauma I experienced. I was sexually abused by my stepfather at 14 and experienced trauma from boys and other men from childhood through young adulthood. I dated men I knew were losers and had nothing promising to offer me. When the married woman found me on the internet, I had become entangled with a man I became obsessed over who presented himself as single. I found out later he was married and separated from his wife. Before finding out he was still married, we quickly became involved and I moved in with him abandoning my own apartment. I fearfully stayed in my apartment for 6 months without leaving it except to go to work, church, and the grocery store after ending my relationship with my eldest child's father, who was physically, emotionally, and sexually abusive. After incubating from a relationship where I was beaten down in the floor and pulled out of a car in front my child and others, I ran into the arms of a secretly married man. This married man was 14 or 15 years older than I was. I believed he was a good candidate for my "happily ever after" solely because of his seniority. Unfortunately, I discovered I was wrong. I essentially was his sex slave even after I found out he was still married. He had kicked me and my daughter out of his home leaving us homeless. He had nothing going for him really except a house and the appearance of being a strong man. I was more stable financially than he was and more driven at 22. Yet, my financial stability paled in comparison to my mental stability. I call my connection with him or anyone who I know brings nothing to the table emotionally or financially except trauma and drama—as "partnering down."

Partnering down was a pattern that was not exclusive to men. The married woman on the internet or my secret lover who wanted me to stop "that" had nothing to offer me as far a stable relationship or companionship. *Zero.* Their thought processes did not challenge me, nor did they pursue their dreams or aspirations. They were content with just existing, which differed for me because I am a driven dreamer. All either of them represented to me was sex. Sexing and partnering down were ways I coped. Let me be clear--these people were mere coping tools for me. If I had realized that fact then, I probably would not be writing this book. If I had known that these encounters were a form of coping with traumatic triggers, I would have seen a therapist sooner (huge pun intended).

In essence, my childish psyche viewed both men and women as sex objects--not people or lovers. It took years of therapy for me to realize I was not a sinner destined for Hell or the fate of Sodom and Gomorrah. I further realized that I was robbed of the normal sexual development that many other children experience, and these experiences negatively affected my view of sex and sexuality. I partnered down because I could control these people because I understood how to play with other's minds sexually, as I had developed this trait at an early age. I believed having a partner, who was beneath me, made me feel in control and less vulnerable. Due to fear of being abused, abandoned, or being labeled gay or weird, I rationalized connecting with (and at times victimizing) these individuals, who displayed their own unhealthy behaviors and coping such as toxicity and manipulation. My rationalization was they were losers, whom I could control, and interacting with them could enable me to hide the dilemma I had about relating to women.

I found through therapy that I rationalized my irrational fear about my sexuality due to my lack of understanding about the difference between sex and sexuality. It was also a result of my unhealthy attempts to mask my past sexual trauma that I believed automatically defined my sexuality. Through careful assessment, my therapist determined that I had a sexual attraction to women but not a romantic one. I did not accept this assessment without carefully researching it myself being the clinical psychologist that I am. Once I did, it made perfect sense. My first sexual experiences were with girls. At an age when other little girls were playing with Barbie dolls, there were some little girls using me as their doll. It stands to reason that I could develop a sexual attraction to a woman given I was introduced sexually to girls at a young age.

Allow me to define sexual attraction and romantic attraction along with sexual orientation. Defining these terms will add further distinction and context as to why I was conflicted in this area in the first place. I say this with certainty given once I gained clarity here, I weaken my fear of judgment that allowed me to journal openly my purest thoughts here with you. *Sexual attraction* (cognitive, erotic, fleshly, carnal) relates to one's desire for sexual contact or sexual interest in another person or other people. *Romantic attraction* (cognitive, emotional, loving, passionate, adoring) leads to one wanting romantic contact with another person or persons. Sexual orientation is a concept that encompasses the variability in one's sexual attraction, romantic attraction, and sexual practices. I developed a sexual attraction to women likely before the age of 8. That's that. Despite that interest, I have a strong romantic attraction toward men.

Because my sexual orientation was perplexing to me before I attended therapy. I thought for years that I had to put my attraction or orientation in a box—gay, lesbian, or bisexual. For me, putting myself in a box (conforming) was a form of self-hate. Self-hatred relates to feeling inadequate and possessing low self-esteem, in this case, feeling inadequate because I do not fit in society's sexuality box. Individuals who demonstrate self-hate compare themselves to other people, focusing on all of their negative qualities, never embracing their positive attributes, holding the belief that they are not good enough, and constantly trying to force themselves into a box. In essence, hating who they are.

Boxes are made by people, which is why I do not like them. If I want to be in a box, I will make my own. I hated how I perceived others would view my sexuality. I felt inadequate because I viewed it as a negative part of me. After years of ignoring it, I came out about my sexuality to my therapist and shared with her my dilemma. I was sick of boxing or masking up my real persona because of shame and being judged. The self-hate about my sexual attraction to women I hid for too long. Unfortunately, that hidden attraction got the best of me on a few occasions when I drank too much. I was always able to use drinking as an excuse for acting on that attraction when I did, until one day it wasn't just a slight misunderstanding. I sexually pursued a woman in the open. I felt the sexual attraction and I went with it as the alcohol removed my inhibitions. It was embarrassing and awkward for us both. Nothing happened except *I was exposed.* The mask was ripped off.

I'm glad the mask got ripped off. It forced me to commit myself to therapy to resolve the internal conflict once and for all about this thing I was hiding. Therapy helped me to realize that my sexual attraction to women only manifested itself when I was sexually frustrated. As long as I had wild or drunken sex with men when I wanted or needed it, the same sex attraction was dormant. I understood sex as love until my therapist helped me to uncover my motivation for having sex. I almost immediately had sex with my male partners when I first met them, or I had sexual encounters with women when I was sexually frustrated. If I could not connect in a romantic way with a man, I fantasized about connecting with a woman, and in the early days acted on that dormant sexual attraction to women. My motivation was my fear that I would not connect to anyone—be it a man or a woman. I did not want to be alone nor did I want to be abandoned.

I discovered at last that my reckless sexual and romantic behaviors were the result of my fear of abandonment. I unconsciously had convinced myself that I was safe from abandonment because I had partnered down. No matter who I was with, though, I was vulnerable because I was clueless as to what drove me internally in either direction. Probably as early as 5 or 6, the fear of abandonment was ingrained into my brain's pathways after my parents separated and later divorced.

Partners, albeit women or men, were objects that I used sexually to feel "loved" and connected to because I developed this mindset from my early sexual encounters. My immature sexual development and social skills made me prey (sometimes predator) in my encounters, while inhibiting me from actually connecting and building a healthy relationship with anyone.

4. Becoming Prey (Neediness)

I am certain that the imaginary "Kick Me" sign was part of the hindrance of me building a healthy relationship. The sign let abusive men know I was easy, needy prey. I could meet someone and feel an intense chemistry and think it was "love at first sight." I would latch on like "Save me, save me!" I would call or text a guy multiple times a day, demand to see him every free moment we had, buy him expensive gifts, and position myself as his caretaker in every way—financially, emotionally, and sexually. Because I assumed the caretaker position of a grown ass man, who typically was emotionally unavailable, we never would connect. The lack of connection, I despised.

My therapist explained why I could not connect. She told me it was an unhealthy attachment style or my pattern of relating to men—that I later discovered was how I related to women also. I was relieved that she did not label me as gay. I do not have a problem with gay people. I had a problem with being in a society that forces you to identify as something even if you do not identify with it. I do not identify as Black, though I use the term at times to communicate with people ignorant about the fact that race is a made-up construct. Look at the color of my caramel skin and look at a color spectrum that includes the color black. Do they match? Look at a "white" person and look at the color spectrum and ask yourself if they match. I made my point. Look at the push on applications and forms to identify one's race and sexuality--heterosexual (straight), homosexual (gay), bisexual, transsexual, pansexual, queer, asexual and so forth. It is the box phenomenon that I shared in an earlier chapter. Ask any person, no matter how he or she identifies sexually, and there are variations to what he or she actually identifies with. Second point made. The push for the identification of sexuality is why I have had numerous teenagers and adults to seek me out for therapy because they were confused about what they are, or rather what box they *should* check. They, too, are traumatized because they live in a society that forces its inhabitants to identify and conform to labels created by dictators and enemies of free will and choice. The scamdemic created even more boxes--mask or no mask, social distancing, or no social distancing. The constant plot to divide us as a society repulses me. The constant divisiveness can be seen in the teenagers who shared their experiences that made them question if they belonged and, if so, where. The mental mind fuckery was in them, just as it was in me, because we hid one simple fact. *We are all here to figure out life on our own terms, but many of us get caught up in fear that if we decided (and openly accepted and expressed that decision) to live our life differently from others we would be outcasted.* Many, who are struggling with this just like I was, feel like they are an alien with three horns on their heads destined for a first-class ticket to the pit of hell or being ostracized from our families, communities, and country of origin.

I digress.

My inability to connect, according to my therapist, was my attachment style. There are four attachment styles--*secure, anxious-preoccupied, dismissing-avoidant,* and *fearfully-avoidant.* Dr. Lisa Firestone, PhD briefly described these styles in her article on Psychology Today called *How Your Attachment Style Impacts Your Relationship.* The *secure attachment style* involves the person allowing himself or herself to connect with a partner and allowing that partner to move freely instead of being too clingy or too avoidant. The individual is able to do so because of the secure attachment that was formed with a parent or caregiver during early development. The other three types are unhealthy attachment styles that resulted from unstable attachment in the course of early development. The *anxious-preoccupied attachment style* entails one, who seeks to be saved or completed, relating to another person for that reason. Hence, the person fantasizes and emotionally craves a partner. The emotional craving causes the person to smother the other by becoming too clingy, ultimately pushing the partner away. The *dismissive-avoidant attachment style*, as the name applies, involves the person acting dismissive toward his or her partner by isolating himself or herself and being emotionally unavailable or avoidant. The person portrays a false independence to avoid becoming too close to the other person, which in the end prevents a healthy partner connection. The *fearfully-avoidant attachment style* is the most conflicted of the unhealthy styles. The person is stuck in the state of ambivalence about being too close or too far away from the other person. Even though, he or she desires the closeness of the relationship. The person reacts to the intense (conflicted or mixed) emotions, like the fear of being hurt or fear of feeling connected, often doing the opposite of what he or she feels. If the person feels the relationship is getting too close, he or she may push the other person away. If the person feels the relationship is fading, he or she may become obsessive and smother the partner not allowing the other person to move freely. The individual's obsession leads to making his or her feeling *too* known or not known at all, which ultimately prevents him or her from getting their emotional needs met.

I was that ambivalent person. I feared getting too close so I would not show my true feelings, or I would be emotionally unavailable if I were pursued by a healthy partner. To keep my feelings hidden, I would engulf myself in work or projects and avoid healthy emotional connections. If a man did something nice for me like give me a compliment, buy me something, or spend a nice evening with me, I would become dismissive and coy or hard and callous. I also would vacillate from callousness to overindulgence, smothering a partner, when I feared that our time would end. It was addictive and polarizing—invigorating when I chased him and gut-wrenching when I didn't. The dichotomous polarity of *"I want you, no I don't really want you"* could happen over weeks or months or it could happen in a single moment communicating with my partner or suitor. Here is a little scenario.

Monday

Him: (Text message.) Hey you.
Me: Hey. What's up? (*Avoiding getting too close.*)
Him: Nothing much. What's up with you?

Me: It's funny. I was just thinking about you. (*Smothering as the adrenaline and dopamine surges.*)

Him: Oh, really.

Me: Yeah. I'm not up to much. Just working on my business and trying to figure out if I'm going out dancing tonight. (*Avoiding getting too close, as I perceive he didn't seem as excited as I felt.*)

Him: You working?

Me: I'm about to finish up. Hey, can I call you? (*Hurrying to avoid being abandoned, I say I'm not busy, though I am, and I ask to switch to a call because I don't want to miss a cue mistakenly through a text message.*)

Him: Sure.

Me: (*Calling immediately once I get his permission.*) Hey, you. (*Overly excited but trying to play calm because I have him on the line.*)

Him: Hey.

Me: So, I was saying I might go dancing. Why are you trying to do something? (*Desperate not to sound desperate but hoping he would ask me out.*)

Him: I was trying to see what you were up to. I was thinking about going to that new restaurant.

Me: Cool. Tonight? (*Smothering.*)

Him: Nah, not tonight. I got some things I need to finish up. I was thinking about Friday or Saturday.

Me: Which one? Friday or Saturday? (*I need concreteness to cope and ensure I am not being abandoned.*)

Him: I don't know yet. It depends on if I get all my errands done.

Me: Oh, I got you. I was just asking because you know I stay busy. I thought you were trying to hang out. I'm not trying to keep you from getting your errands done. (*Emotionally distressed, I abandon myself before he can say 'no,' but I am hoping my dismissive response will trigger him to reassure me that he won't abandon me.*)

Him: I should have them done before Friday, but I'll let you know.

Me: Well, I'll let you go. I know you're busy, and you'll let me know on Friday. (*I am abandoning myself again from the call to keep him from ending it, which would make me feel more abandoned, though still feel desperate and abandoned.*)

Him: You're good. We'll talk later.

Me: (Texting two days later) I'm looking forward to Friday (*I sent a text message because he said "later," but he did not specify how much later. It's been two days, and I want to make sure he knows I'm still interested. The text message sounds smothering* to me, so I follow it with a smiley emoji that suggests I'm not attached--just being a cool chick.)

Him: Cool. (*Overwhelmed because I don't know if this message means we are still on for Friday.*)

Me: (*Reading all the text messages to ensure I didn't say something weird and replaying our entire phone conversation, fearing Friday we won't get together.*)

Friday

Me: (*Looking at my phone to make sure the ringer is on and checking text messages to ensure I did not miss the call throughout the day.*)

Him: (Early afternoon text) Hey, does 7 tonight work?

Me: (Immediately when the message is received) Sure where are we meeting? (*I sit through my remaining appointments nervous and stressed hoping that something awful does not happen before 7. I abandon anything else I may have committed to. I yell at traffic as I stress that I will not make it on time, and he leaves. I arrive early and sit in my car until 7 playing it cool.*)

That dialogue is the mind fuckery of a fearful avoidant. My attachment style not only complicated how I interact with a partner but also what type of partner I attracted. This type of guy only comes around when he wants to come around. If I initiated the encounter, he likely does not respond. He is the type that occasionally wants companionship. When we hang out, we have an amazing time though while having a good time I fear abandonment because I know he is the abandoning type. I abandon myself by even going out with this kind of man. I am driven to these types because of the intense fear of having someone who might be healthy abandoning me--someone who would actually show up consistently. I remember the last night me and this guy was together. I cried in my pillow lying next to him as he slept overcome with fear that he would go M.I.A. the next day like he had down multiple times in the past. The way I interested relates to how I interpreted my parents' divorce and all the uncertainties that came with that as abandonment. I taught myself to vacillate between being too attached to not being attached at all to my parents or anyone for that matter to avoid the emotional pain of the *fear* of abandonment. I was being that same little girl lying in the bed with this man. The small child who believed, based on her limited understanding, that if your parents abandon you, then so will a man. Before my intense two years of therapy, I told myself men were dogs, abusive, and dramatic, and I was their prey. The fact was *the men I dated* were this way, not all men, and I was dramatic as well until I started dating myself. That earlier scenario went on and on for years with different men creating an addictive, debilitating experience called *re-traumatization.*

5. Wanting Closure (Low Self-Worth)

Re-traumatization is experiencing trauma again and again whether it is actual trauma or ruminating on past traumatic events. I was in three car accidents in 2014 that resulted in a lifetime of chronic pain. My orthopedic specialist told me that typically it is not the injury that causes the most pain but the re-injury of the injury that causes chronic pain and debilitation. Every time I turned suddenly, reached up too high, or lifted something too heavy, I re-injured myself. Likewise, it was not those initial traumas I experienced in childhood, whether at the babysitter's or my relative's home, that injured me the most. It was the re-injury of that *trauma* that crippled me. Over and over again I inflicted emotional and psychological pain on myself due to lack of self-awareness that I was retraumatizing myself and my having low self-worth. I did not know *what I did not know.* I showed up to relationships feeling like a piece of shit enabling predators to re-injure me, like a piece of shit. I kept the wounds open. Although my re-traumatization and the behaviors associated with them were reckless, it leads me to closure about how these things through my dating journey.

Closure is a funny thing many humans seek when they experience a loss. Loss involves grieving. David Kessler, who is the world expert on grief describes it in five stages—denial, anger, bargaining, depression, and acceptance. In terms of grief, closure relates to what Kessler describes as bargaining. Bargaining takes the form of the person postulating "what ifs" about what happened and what he or she could have done differently. It is intense studying of the past or ruminating to rationalize a loss and how we contributed to it. Unfortunately, trying to undo the past through bargaining causes more emotional distress. After a traumatic experience or a breakup, a person may seek closure about it. Seeking closure, though, is problematic and usually causes more distress. Whatever reasons we are given for the event, we start to rationalize ways we can fix those reasons to undo the loss. That rationalization is a mental comfort we attempt to provide ourselves rather than facing the emotional discomfort of the lost.

I sought closure each time I had a "breakup," even if it was a one-night stand, often to the point of insanity. If it were not for therapy, I would have never received *real* closure because the closure I was seeking was closure from my past. I wanted someone to explain to the little girl why years later those encounters would still affect her. I needed to know how to undo the damage that was done. I wanted to know if the other persons were suffering, too. I wanted them to tell that little girl she was *worth not hurting.* Since I could not or wouldn't ask them, I looked in the darkest emotional places I could find—traumatic relationships—to bandage ("close") the wound. Many men told me I was worth it. Their kind words were useless to me given I did not accept my own worth. As soon as I would make what I felt was a connection, I envisioned our whole lives together in bliss. Then, when bliss was a nightmare, I confirmed in myself: "See, you're a piece of shit; you're worthless; that's why they abandoned you."

Imagine every day from childhood to entering middle-age, waking up and interacting with people believing you are a real worthless piece of shit. You treat not only yourself like a piece of shit; you treat everyone else like a piece of shit. I covered up my low self-worth well by being the first to help other people, especially in my career. But the real piece-of-shit-me showed up in my personal relationships. It was me avoiding emotional connections with my kids at times because I was overwhelmed by the great love, they showed me, which I did not know how to respond to. It was me being resentful toward my mother for years telling myself she was never satisfied with me. It was me marrying two men, believing I was totally prepared for love, yet showing up every day like an emotional psycho loving them at one moment and literally hating them the next. It took years and months of me working through the trauma to articulate what this *fractured mind* had conceived was reality and differentiating those conceptions with truth. I conceived that being the piece of shit that I was, I was destined to be treated like a piece of shit. The truth was that if I only expected shit, then I would only get shit, and I always had a reason to end it all--a life filled with shit. When I admitted this truth to myself, I realized why I felt so unworthy. It was not because of something that happened in childhood. It was because I woke up every day and created a personal reality of shitty unworthiness. This was my closure and my movement in the grief process straight to acceptance. It was not trauma or my abusers that made me unworthy. It wasn't my past *per se* either. It was my drive to cover up my shame (re-trauma) about a nonexistent past (trauma) in fear of exposing that past (re-trauma) in my future all the while sabotaging (re-trauma) the beauty of my present.

6. Hypersexuality (Infatuation)

My sabotage was the lack of self-awareness and self-acceptance about my pure expression of sexuality masked with fake personas. I am asking my voice right now, how much you, the reader, really needs to know about my sexuality (Hold one moment: I'm downloading. . .). Sabotage or self-sabotage is a tricky and difficult thing that I manifested through infatuation. It was my addiction of choice. I have shared with my followers on Facebook and Instagram (@followdrdeee) that I am addicted to alcohol and currently living a life of recovery. I've shared little, until now, about my infatuation addiction. As an addict and psychologist, I know that addiction is not about the substance or activity but rather one's *cognitive response to the chemicals produced in the brain's reward/pleasure-seeking pathway through the repetitive use of a substance or engagement in an activity.* The repetitive use of a drug, for example, along with behaviors associated with the drug use increases the release of dopamine in an addict. While an individual naturally can experience the release of dopamine from fulfilling primal needs such as food, water, and sex, an addict over time has caused changes to occur in his or her brain that permanently alter its pleasure-seeking pathway. Thus, the occasional romantic infatuations or alcohol binges at a young age eventually led to the development of a brain disease that caused me to seek out real or imagined sexual or romantic relationships and develop a love-hate relationship with alcohol as I chased the recurrence of that first sexual and alcoholic high.

Craig Nakken in *The Addictive Personality* calls the type of high I was chasing the "satiation" high. He indicated that this type of high makes the addict feel complete and free from experiencing physical or emotional pain. The addict feels this opioid pain relief until he or she comes down from the high. Once the high mood is gone, the addict feels grief. To numb the original pain that the grief causes, the addict uses again. The addict becomes an addict because he or she does this repeatedly developing a cycle of addictive behaviors. Experiencing emotional pain from the fear of abandonment and sexual confusion, I became infatuated with sex, often along with alcohol, to numb my pain. The infatuated behavior, as Nakken suggested, took control over me as I believed that just the right dose of my drug could take away all the pain.

My infatuation (addiction) to men and our reckless rendezvous temporarily numbed my fear of abandonment as it turned out. Psychology refers to this type of addiction as *hypersexuality*. Hypersexuality, or compulsive sexual behavior, is an abnormal excessive preoccupation with or indulgence in sexual activity such as sexual fantasies, behaviors, or distress that negatively affect an individual's functioning in an area of life like a job or relationships. I would love to say that hypersexuality for me was just fantasy, but it encompassed all three components. When I felt I was getting too close to someone, I would isolate myself and have daily fantasies throughout the day, and particularly at night, about sex and our phone conversations (remember how I obsessed over the text messages in Chapter 3?). Men primarily would fill these fantasies, but women would compulsorily fill them when I was sexually frustrated because I hadn't had sex with a man in a while. I would experience intense distress because of my Christian upbringing for fantasizing at all but especially about my fantasies about women.

So, I never told anyone.

I would rationalize *righting* this Christian *wrong* secretly, trying to erase my abomination, by seeking "the man of my dreams" to make an honest or *real* woman out of me. I would go on the wagon and hide in my home for 6 months at a time, only going to work and church. During this time, I would read my Bible, just to come out of hiding to find myself falling into another awful relationship or one-night stand--wrong again. I became more addicted through this self-sabotage. I drank to numb feeling like a whore. I had addictive sex to numb myself from the reality that I lacked skills to form a healthy connection. I feared something that was supposed to be beautiful—my sexuality. I was perplexed for a time on how I could help clients overcome this cycle being stuck in my own. Being stuck, dating was not dating at all until I really put in the therapeutic work for myself. Now, I can help my clients do the same--let go of their self-sabotage, that is, their self-abandonment.

7. Self-abandonment (Defense Mechanism)

The revelation of my self-abandonment was ironic, considering that every coping strategy I used was to *avoid* any type of abandonment. Susan Anderson, in her book *Taming the Outer Child,* wrote that an adult cannot be abandoned. From her book, I came to understand that the intense feeling that I feared wasn't being abandoned, but rather I was afraid of *the feeling of abandonment.*

None of my lovers could abandon the adult "me," if I acted like one. I showed up to these consensual encounters and co-signed for the recklessness, triggering the dreaded feeling myself. I tried to avoid an emotion (feeling of abandonment) believing I was preventing an action (abandonment). I created the self-abandonment longing to fill a deep emotional need—to feel and be loved and protected. I did not know what being loved and protected meant or how to gain either in a healthy way. I learned to tame that outer infatuated child and began acting like an adult to explore, understand, and embrace love.

While learning to embrace love, I had to overcome the sea of infatuation. In infatuation, I experienced love at some time, I am sure. And I am just as certain that I rejected it. I turned down healthy suitors who tried taking things slow and working toward commitment. I would look down on them saying "He's not my type." What I meant was, "He doesn't stimulate me or get me high." His lack of stimulation (or inability to send surges of dopamine to my brain) thrust me into other vicious cycles of looking for "Mr. Right," but always partnering down with "Mr. *Right Now*." I felt worthy under the Mr. Right Now-induced dopamine highs, but when the high was over, I suffered from withdrawal and felt unlovable at a near suicide level every time. Withdrawal symptoms for me were changes in appetite, headaches, muscle tension, sexual frustration, depression, inability to concentrate, and suicidal ideations. Not so surprisingly, these were the same symptoms I had withdrawing from alcohol. Yet, I drank lethal amounts of alcohol to numb myself from the dopamine withdrawal. The more I chased the DOPE-a-mine, the more I drank. I hope the picture is clear that I was the abandoner of self.

Seeking to eliminate my abandonment of self, I pursued a better way to—get this—love myself. Social media and mainstream media promote love as a destination. Think of your news feeds. They are filled with posts and snapshots from individuals professing that they arrived. *"I found my true love,"* one post read. *Destination.* Chick flicks employ a plot centered around its characters arriving at love, their capacity to stay in love, or their inability to find love--as if love has direct coordinates. *Destination.* Instead of promoting love as a destination, loving of one's self should be the goal daily. Giving self-love daily equates to believing and doing for one's self those things that bring a sense of emotional wholeness.

Self-love is believing one is worthy of positive things such as achieving goals, having new and unique experiences, and developing fulfilling relationships, and seeking those good things. It is the individual who manifests or demonstrates the love to himself or herself first before seeking love from another. Through self-love, the individual can connect in a healthy way with another human being and interact with that person in the spirit of worthiness. I showed up to relationships feeling unworthy and seeking to be made worthy. I joined others' worlds looking to be completed. This self-defeating attitude resulted in the sense of feeling incomplete. We all are born with the capacity to create and develop, and that capacity is determined by the Creator--not the created. There is no way you or I can complete another created human being. Yet, we can create a sense of mental wholeness in terms of how we value ourselves and our ability to connect with others. Understanding the need for mental wholeness was the truth that broke my cycle of abandonment. I decided to spend my remaining years I have here on Earth dating myself. (That sounds so sexy). I could dress up in heels with a thigh-dress or do a 5-mile walk and 100 pushups for myself. I could attend my own therapy, like I encourage my clients to do, for myself. I could choose to live whole by refusing to allow fear and addiction to control my life.

Thus, I denounced my addiction to sex and alcohol. I still like sex, but my motivation for it is different. My motivation for sex now is to express my self-love that can mean long periods of abstinence. No more sexing the first or second night or even a kiss for that matter to alleviate the possibility of entanglements. No more mind fucks; it was time for healing.

Part II: Exposing the Self

Concentrate all your thoughts upon the work in hand. The sun's rays do not burn until brought to a focus.

~Alexander Graham Bell~

8. Healing (Restoration of Self)

Healing or restoring myself was necessary after dismissing a mental cancer--like self-abandonment. Cancer survivors strive to keep the disease in full remission, and so do I. The little girl who was abandoned in childhood could no longer show up to dates, interpersonal relationships, or the world waiting for mommy, daddy, or superman to swoop down and save her. That behavior is cancerous. Rather, the adult me reported to the work of healing to gain further knowledge of my triggers and vices that may inhibit my recovery and residual effects of trauma. Healing restored my self-awareness, which I used to bring my*self back* to life.

My lack of awareness was a negative effect of past trauma called dissociation, *the disintegration from self that can occur as the brain attempts to protect an individual from trauma*. It is a mental escape. While this experience may have been useful to me and trauma victims during our traumatic experiences, it often can handicap us later in life when the trauma is no longer present. Derealization, depersonalization, and dissociative amnesia are three common types of dissociation. I typically experience all three.

Depersonalization, the dissociation I experience the most, is the feeling of observing one's self outside of one's own body. Imagine a small child who is sexually assaulted feeling defenseless against someone who is physically larger than him or her or who is in a position of authority. The child's brain responds to the trauma by choosing mentally to escape from that reality. If the abuse is habitual, the brain may *escape* from reality multiple times. As the child's brain develops, it may cause the child to depersonalize unconsciously to escape distress related to trauma or perceived trauma in later life. In my experience as a victim of sexual abuse, I would leave my body routinely. I did not become aware of these mental escapes until I went through therapy, even though I was trained as a psychologist to recognize this coping strategy in others. For example: I almost never had sex with anyone without being drunk or high. I discovered through my healing and sobriety that I often would drink excessively before I expected to have sex. I drank to mask the feelings of guilt and shame that were a result of consciously violating my Christian upbringing. More importantly, I drank to prevent myself from being aware of being outside of my body. If I did not drink, which was rare, I would fantasize about having sex with someone or multiple people other than the person I was having sex with to prevent myself from *looking* at myself from outside myself as sex felt traumatic even though I wanted to have sex. Clients with past trauma also report outer body experiences similar to this as well.

Understanding my outer body experiences and other dissociative experiences were paramount to my healing. In order to show up for myself, I had to gain awareness of other instances besides sex where I left my body or got lost in my mind. To my surprise, I spent much of my conscious time in a mental fog where I was in the world but did not seem to be a part of it. This is called derealization. I could be among family and friends talking and interacting yet feel like I am in a time warp and not actually there. My rational mind knew I was there, but I felt like a ghost going through the motions instead of me being mentally present.

Going through the motions, I experienced lapses in time while I was working, talking, reading, or watching television. I was detached from these things without knowing it. My inability to remember saying something to my kids or doing an activity is known as dissociative amnesia, another form of dissociation. This was probably the most frustrating for me and most difficult to cope with. I have spoken matter-of-factly for as long as I could remember. I describe this style of speech as making sure the person to whom I am speaking has all the details, but it was me trying to recall all the details I could not remember. I could not simply share with a friend I had enjoyed going to new restaurant, for example. I had to tell them every thought and action that I experienced to include how I ate my food. My friends thought I was talkative. I found out I was trying not to forget.

Not forgetting, staying in my body, and clearing the fog is why I committed in 2020 to living in the present. The act of remaining or focusing on the present is called mindfulness, which is rooted in the acceptance and commitment therapy (ACT). ACT espouses that individuals face their thoughts and feelings instead of going out of their way to avoid them or feeling guilty about them. ACT also postulates that avoiding intense emotions causes even more intense emotions that compound that first uncomfortable emotion. For instance, a person who feels anxious and tries to avoid that anxiety may begin to feel guilty about feeling anxious. He or she then may feel sad about feeling guilty, and that sadness may result in angry feelings caused by sadness about the guilt felt when she was anxious. It is clearly a destructive situation that feeds on itself.

Regarding mindfulness, I regularly teach and use it to help myself and clients learn to overcome the emotional rollercoaster and live in the moment. When I am distressed by my thoughts, I use my five senses to distract myself from my intrusive thoughts and bring myself back to the present moment. I ask myself "What do I see? What do I hear? What do I taste? What do I feel? What do I smell?" Additionally, I will take deep breaths counting to ten as I inhale each breath and counting to ten as I exhale. In less than five minutes, I usually can bring myself back to the present moment. After practicing, I find myself in a state of control and calm, making myself aware that I can let my thoughts flow and not overpower me by focusing on what is right in front of me. Mindfulness is just one of the ways I restore myself and practice healing. *(Visit https://azzerturself.com/webinar for access to my "Mindfulness for Control" training video.)*

Healing is an ongoing, dynamic process. I chuckle when clients ask me "How long does it take to heal, Dr. D?" as if a person can learn how to heal emotional wounds in a set time and way. Healing is a mindset, not an end point. The eerie fear of abandonment can come at any time, particularly in the initial healing process. Be mindful that a healing moment does not necessarily carry over, just as exercising today doesn't guarantee you will be fit tomorrow. You need practice. My healing includes acknowledging when past hurt may have triggered negative thoughts, feelings, and behaviors in the present. It requires me to reframe and change those negative thoughts to reflect what is happening in the moment. For instance, I may go on a date and feel anxious as I fear abandonment. My mind begins to wonder if I am saying all the right things and wonder what will happen tomorrow or next year regarding the relationship. At that time, I must accept that these thoughts and feelings are based on excessive worry about the future and over concern about my past. Neither the future nor past exists—just the present. With acceptance, I begin to realize that although I cannot predict the future nor change my past, I have some control over the present. I can focus on the dinner we are eating and stay in the moment, bringing myself back into my body and mind with my "What do I see, hear, taste, feel, and smell" routine. I realize that I had taken a short trip and my date never knew I left. I may never stop dissociating, but I can choose how I will respond to dissociation when it occurs. That's the beauty of healing; you can choose to heal.

Other strategies I choose to practice in my healing include journaling, writing (including this soon-to-be best-selling book), exercising, energy work, setting and maintaining boundaries, and valuing myself. Owning my value means avoiding addictive behaviors, toxic people, and self-sabotage. Avoiding these behaviors means living a sober life. Sobriety means I must refrain from chasing unnatural dopamine highs and pursue natural highs that take a bit more work and are usually harder to experience initially, but worth my healing. Healing requires more than sober living and eliminating addiction; it requires forgiving yourself and others.

Practical Healing Activity:

Reappraisal journaling is a written cognitive restructuring or evaluation of a perceived emotionally eliciting event or stressor in a way that promotes healthy resolution of the emotion or stressor. Rather than avoiding what is feared, I help my clients face what they fear through mental exposure. Find a quiet room or space where you feel comfortable where there are no distractions. Turn your cell phone on do not disturb. Set your phone timer to 5 minutes. (You can increase that time to 10 minutes as you become more comfortable doing this activity). Go to YouTube, search for, and play relaxing spa music. My favorite type of relaxing music has water or harp sounds. You can choose the spa music you like. Start the timer and close your eyes. Take 3 deep breaths, inhaling slowly and deeply through your nose to the count of ten and exhaling slowly to the count of ten out of your mouth. Begin to focus on what scares you the most. Picture every detail, what it looks like, feels like, smells like, words you may hear, and even tastes you may experience. Imagine that it is actually happening in this moment. As soon as you get this picture in your mind, imagine all the ways you can solve what you are afraid of as if you have a human superpower. When the timer stops, write down your experience. Be sure to include all that you were afraid of and all that you were able to resolve about the fear. Reframe your feelings about all that you envisioned as you experienced the event in your mind and survived it. Write extensively about how you feel about surviving your greatest fear. Do this activity whenever you are fearful or anxious. Keep this journal entry as a reminder in a safe place as a reminder of your strength. Label it "My Strength."

9. Forgiveness (Blame No One)

Forgiveness requires not playing the blame game. I ranted on a post I wrote on Facebook some time ago about entertainers Will Smith and Jada Pinkett-Smith that she had had an "entanglement" with another man during her marriage. She and Will discussed their marriage and her entanglement on her Facebook program—the Red Table Talk show. My post on Facebook was titled "Infidelity Exposed!" in which I shared my own story about infidelity. The point of my post was to show that playing the blame game is just another victim tactic that does not resolve anything. I wanted people to understand that things happen, and that you do not have to wait for Will and Jada or some other famous person to speak up about their drama to deal with your own. How you live and deal with your problems is up to you.

I deal with problems at times holding grudges, and other times I chose forgiveness. I favor forgiveness because it is therapeutic and healing. The problem is few people really understand what forgiveness is. Forgiveness is a one-person act that involves letting go of the right to sentence someone for offending or hurting you. To be honest, it's actually deeper than that. It is letting go of sentencing yourself to bitterness and anger that would otherwise seep through your emotional pores into your relationship with yourself and others the same way processed meat seeps through your pores (yuck). The great thing about forgiveness is it takes only you.

Here is what I mean. Imagine being stopped for speeding, and the police officer gives you a ticket for reckless driving. You go to court to fight the ticket, but the officer provides evidence that shows you are without a doubt guilty. You believe that after the officer's testimony, you are going to get the largest fine and stiffest penalty—including losing your license. The judge looks you straight in the eye and says, "I'm going to let you off with a warning." That is forgiveness.

But "Wait," the judge says as you start to walk out of the courtroom "you cannot have any more moving violations, or I'll revoke your license. You have to come back to this courtroom in two years so I can see if you have had any other violations." That is called reconciliation, and it requires two people. This is where people get confused. Reconciliation occurs when two or more people decide to agree to restore their relationship to a certain status. When people hold grudges, they may be conflicted, not knowing whether to forgive the other person as they mistake forgiveness for reconciliation. Thus, they hang on to the grudge allowing it to fester emotionally. Letting go of a grudge does not mean you are reconciling because reconciliation requires conditions; forgiveness does not. Forgiveness is given freely without conditions. I have learned in the healing process that it was not as difficult as I thought to forgive others. *What was difficult was to forgive myself.* Will and Jada talked about working through there entanglement and other challenges in their marriage. They talked a lot about talking through their feelings and internal conflict. They never explicitly talked about forgiveness, but they talked intensely about reconciliation. Maybe Will and Jada forgive each other and themselves and did not share it. I am being intentional in explaining that the effective formal for healing is forgiveness and if possible, reconciliation--not in the opposite order.

Here is the "Infidelity Exposed" Facebook post, slightly paraphrased for clarity, where I essentially was talking through my own forgiveness of myself and hoping to inspire others to do the same.

Infidelity Exposed!

Will and Jada are talking about it at the red table.

It's nothing new.

It happens.

I don't think many people grow up *planning* to marry and then cheat on their spouse.

Most clients I counsel on infidelity think infidelity starts the moment someone has sex with someone other than his or her partner.

Infidelity, though, starts in the heart.

I was married for 14 years to someone who wasn't faithful before the marriage.

I thought I loved him enough to make him love me and only me. After all, I gave him children.

I remember the first time I heard the key turn in the lock after a night he didn't come home. I had called him over and over again, but no answer. I knew he was cheating.

When I looked into his eyes as he walked into the living room the next morning, it was confirmation.

I cried, fought, cursed, threw shit, and damn near tried to literally kill him.

None of this took away the pain I felt inside.

That event started a vicious cycle.

He cheated more.

I became lonely and emotionally despondent.

I saw someone in the mall one day who smiled and said kind words to me.

This caused an emotional entanglement. It was an emotional affair.

It was an addiction, an addiction to feeling connected to someone while disconnected...an unhealthy connection.

I never had sex with this man, but I gave him my heart and time because I needed to feel less despondent.

It helped me drown out the pain of rejection from the man I committed to love for life temporarily.

When my husband became aware of that emotional affair, he became jealous.

[My husband] started showing me what I thought was love. He defended me by marching to that man's job to tell him never to contact his wife again. (We were both young, dumb, and impulsive).

It was gangsta, nonetheless.

Or was it?

It gave us a short honeymoon, but it didn't change anything.

He still couldn't commit to just love me and showing up for me.

It was 14 years of entanglement.

It wasn't the last time he cheated. He had many women. It wasn't the last time I cheated.

We had kids.

I stayed to save face, to create a perfect family life, not to bear the shame, all the while I lost myself.

I eventually left.

I remarried.

And I was fully committed to my second husband.

We loved each other and supported one another.

I trusted him emotionally.

Then I shared with him a sexual desire I had because up to that point he was emotionally safe.

I had never *done* anything emotionally, sexually, or otherwise to breach his trust.

I was expecting him to have a conversation with me about my desire, and WE would decide what--if anything--**we** would do about that desire.

I was 100% vulnerable with this man, something I wasn't in my first marriage.

From that moment, he became insecure and treated me unfairly. He often trapped me emotionally after this.

I pleaded with him for months for the emotional safety I once felt with him. I assured him over and over again of my faithfulness, and I asked him not to destroy the relationship we had built because of his insecurities.

But I finally reached my breaking point.

I decided to do what he kept accusing me of. I was angry and at the same time exhausted. To be frank, I was pissed!

I felt like what's the point of sharing who you are and what you desire with someone you love if he only uses that information to reject you repeatedly.

In hindsight, I should have left, but I was too scared to be alone and too scared to start over again.

This created more unhappiness for us both.

What I am sharing with you folks is that Will and Jada are people.

I'm a person.

There are a ton of things that I do well, but I'm not perfect.

I'm excellent at counseling and coaching clients in relationships--not because I've ever had a perfect relationship, but because I have good insight, and I tell the truth.

Every time I share my story with a couple who has experienced infidelity, it brings about healing to them both.

I don't regret anything I just told you. I learn from my life's experiences. I'm finally learning *me*.

This isn't school. I don't care how you grade me. I'm in the trenches with myself.

If you spent more time focusing on you, instead of focusing on other people's issues, you might learn something, too.

Will and Jada interest most of you because they don't fear what people think of them--and they forgive themselves.

Your fear of being exposed is what entraps you in a poor quality of life.

I'm not glorifying infidelity.

I'm glorifying the healthiest BOUNDARY you can set for yourself. TELL. THE. TRUTH.

Writing that post was therapeutic for me. People may think I write my posts for them. But they are for me. It is a way I expose or disclose myself. When we expose ourselves, we don't have to wear personas because we're not hiding who we are. The more you disclose the less likely you are to fear being exposed. Exposing one's self is a manifestation of forgiveness. Forgiveness means accepting one's shortcomings, choices, and one's self. In order to align with another, you must have self-acceptance about who you are, what you have or haven't done, and experiences you my had. Self-acceptance is a core value of restoration and healing.

Practical Healing Activity:

Take out a blank sheet of paper and write the letters A through Z down the left side of the page. Close your eyes for a minute and remember that forgiveness is a one-person act that leads to restoration and healing. Also remember that it is impossible to forgive anyone else if you do not forgive yourself first. Now, open your eyes and write an item that starts with each letter of the alphabet that you need to forgive yourself for. An example for A may be *Anger – I forgive myself for every time I became angry with myself for being afraid.* Once your list is complete, take the next 26 days, picking a letter a day, in alphabetical order answering the following questions:

- How has lack of forgiveness in this area affected your emotions, behaviors, relationships, view of yourself and others, and overall quality of life?
- What are the costs and benefits of you forgiving yourself in this area?
- Without deciding whether or not to forgive yourself, write what your life would be like if you **did** forgive yourself.

- Chose now whether you will complete the one-person act of forgiveness for the items you wrote on your list, knowing that daily you choose whether to forgive or not.

10. Self-acceptance (Celebrate Your Flaws)

Choosing to accept yourself is a complex concept called self-acceptance. The concept should be complex just as you are a complex being. You are not a machine. You are a beacon of light that shines differently from every other beacon of light. The challenge is you probably compare yourself to other light. Comparing yourself to something of unequal measure distorts your understanding of yourself. Self-acceptance is the awareness and welcoming of *all* of your worth as a beacon of light, including your great qualities, perceived shortcomings, subjective assessment of your gifts, and potential to accomplish what you desire. It also includes your overall life satisfaction about your past, present, and future. Like I said, it is complex.

Average people get so caught up in the complexity of their unique expressions of light that they diminish their life satisfaction. Rather than getting caught up in their perceived hang-ups (negative evaluations), they should celebrate them. Celebrate your flaws or hang-ups. It is what makes your light so unique. As I write this, I am smiling again. *If I had accepted this concept years ago, how beautiful life would have been at that time.* Thankfully, I can celebrate them all now. I can celebrate that I was introduced to sex at a young age. It means that I'm a damn good lover. I can celebrate cheating on my husbands, not because cheating is cool, but rather because having cheated I have learned to leave any relationship that does not fulfill me. I can celebrate my years of addiction because it makes living in sobriety worth every moment. I can celebrate all of me by sharing my story (without a mask or persona) with the world and seeing how countless lives have changed because I came out of hiding.

As a part of my healing, I gave up alcohol and began attending Alcoholics Anonymous (AA). I rejected the idea for years, thinking I was better than other addicts. I was surprised to find out when I joined that all other addicts thought the same thing about themselves. My first meeting I was introduced to acceptance in a way I have never heard before. It changed the trajectory of my life and how I viewed other people. One of the greatest passages from the AA Big Book says, ". . . acceptance is the answer to *all* my problems today. When I am disturbed, it is because I find some person, place, thing, or situation—some fact of my life—*unacceptable to me* [emphasis added], and I can find no serenity until I accept that person, place, thing, or situation as being exactly the way it is supposed to be at this moment." That passage was the answer to all my problems. All these years I was disturbing myself. It wasn't the past abuse causing the disturbance. It was me not accepting that the abuse was just as it was supposed to be at that moment. Hear me out. I am not encouraging anyone to abuse anyone. Abuse is wrong, and it is illegal. What I am saying and encouraging you to do is to accept that not everything goes our way and to understand that we may have been conditioned to believe that life is supposed to be a certain way. That conditioning caused me to suffer most of my life. I now choose to start every day that I wake up accepting myself for who I am and all that I experience.

I was able to choose accepting myself a few days after hearing that passage by reflecting on the passage itself. I was out shopping with my son and had an experience. A woman quickly squeezed in between me and a shelf to grab something without excusing herself. I felt rage building up and was about to share a few bold words with her. Instead, I began saying out loud "Acceptance is the answer to all my problems today." I said it back-to-back three times rapidly before my son asked if I was okay. I told him "Acceptance is the answer to all my problems today," saying that phrase again. He laughed (as I had shared this phrase with him the day I first heard it), and he said laughing, "Okay, mom." Less than two minutes after the rude woman left, I was able to reclaim my sanity and enjoy the time with my son. In the past, I would have felt bad and questioned myself after I fussed or cussed out someone like that woman, and that I would have wasted a ton of energy. I only needed enough energy to remind myself of what I was in control of—acceptance.

Prior to completing this book, I was dating someone. I have had a few good dates and a ton of bad ones prior to dating this guy. In the past, as I shared, the fear of abandonment would have me acting in ways that did not manifest self-acceptance. Dating him looked like me accepting him and the way he presented himself when we were interacting. I did not try to manipulate our interaction or change him in any way. When I did not what I experienced, I accepted it and I dealt with it. I did not run from it or smother myself in it. This made the dating experience more fun and controllable as I was not dating trying to avoid an irrational fear. After about two months, I felt we were not compatible. I told him and ended our dating agreement not giving into fear or abandoning myself.

The AA Big Book, I believe addresses the addicts irrational fear, as it further says, "I need to concentrate not so much on what needs to be changed in the world as on what needs to be changed in me and my attitudes." I couldn't change that me and that guy were incompatible, but I could change how I responded to the lack of compatibility. I cannot change how you or the world views me, I can only change how I view myself. Fearing the world and situations in the past caused me to have an attitude problem for years. I have dealt with that attitude problem through acceptance. I accept everything about me-- some days it seems to be a little more challenging than others, but I still begin and end it with acceptance. How about you? Even when those quirky smothering traits show up out of nowhere, I accept them. I talk my way through them and share them when appropriate. I move on accepting only what needs to be changed in me. In that moment, if I am rejected by another, I accept in me that person is not for me. I recover and move on quicker this way. This self-acceptance thing is a superpower.

Many people lose their superpower because they received negative feedback from other people along the way. Those other people could have been parents, teachers, lovers, friends, and yes you guess it—mass media. I discussed extensively in my book

From the Voice of a Fractured Mind: Speak Loud the self-defeating core beliefs "I am a flawed me" and "I have to please others." Possessing any other belief than you are a perfect beacon of light is flawed or faulty thinking. You cannot change what you are. In contrast, understanding that you may possess some ineffective or underdeveloped character traits is a problem you can address through skill development and practice. Societal programming has caused many to believe that an underdeveloped skill makes them either "good" or "bad" when in fact we're both. It just depends on what you or I am doing with what we have and whose opinions we give weight in our lives. I have made the executive decision as the Chief Executive officer of my life that the final opinion belongs to me. If you are reading this book and thinking "Dr. D is bad," it is not something I will give weight to--I own the final opinion *remember?* That is how I exercise my superpower. In the past, I would have tried to justify to you to try to change your opinions of me. I've already accepted that I am good and yet I am ole so bad. It is because I am bad that I can recognize my good. *Make sense?*

You can use this same psychological prescription I your life. Refuse to reject your bad and learn to embrace your good.

Use your superpower of self-acceptance. Accept every perceived flaw about yourself by writing them down. Once you write them down, review the list and see how good those bad qualities really are. For example, I used to lie and make up stories to stay out of trouble when I was a kid not just to other people but to myself. It made me more creative. I used to write poetry and fiction stories allowing my imagination to run wild. I am writing this book, though not fiction, that requires me to use my creativity to color my story with words for you to engage, relate, and understand it. You need a pretty big imagination if you want to accomplish anything while you are on this planet—it's called vision. I can still see myself sitting at my desk in my bedroom as a teenager writing a romance novel on a word processor. (I thought I was writing a bestseller). I started getting writer's block one day and, on that day, I realized I did not like writing fiction. I could have given up writing, but as you can see, I am still writing. My superpower is accepting what I am and living out that value.

Practical Healing Activity:

What if you were supposed to have all your flaws? What if those flaws made you unique? What if those flaws are just what the world needs to experience true light and love? What if there is no alternative to those flaws because they were put there by design? What if you celebrated all of this? Write your responses to each of these questions and then buy yourself a cake, does not matter the size, just buy the cake. Eat every bit of that cake. You can share it if you like, but you make sure you get the biggest piece. Put a candle or candles on it if you want to. Add an extra cake decoration. This is your birthday celebration as this is the first time you are celebrating the real you. Mark this day on the calendar and celebrate it as often as you like. Happy Birthday!

11. Date Yourself First (Embrace Self-Worth)

I am a person of value, and I focus on that value or worth daily. *Dating myself* first helps me to do that. I remember going on numerous dates where I would spend hours showering, shaving, putting on makeup, purchasing new clothes, singing 30 playlists, and showing up as if my date had paid for the most expensive escort service in town. I would be sure to eat properly, drink sparingly (or so I thought), and compliment freely. Once the dust settled, and my date vanished after one or two dates or I scared him away, I would break up with myself. I would shower, but I would not spend hours pampering myself like I did when I dated a guy. I internally rationalized this behavior as me embracing my natural beauty. In actuality, it was the display of lack of motivation a person experiences when he or she is depressed. I would feel hopeless that make up and dressy clothes could serve any purpose in my life at that moment. During one of my weekly sessions, as I rambled all the details to my therapist about my sabotaging behavior and my utter hopelessness about ever getting it right, she said "What would it look like if you showed up for yourself?"

(Light bulb.)

People may view me as exempt from experiencing trauma or dealing with conflict because I am a psychologist. Real life problems happen to real people. I am a real person. I like many others never considered showing up for myself. I believed that if I said a little less or little more, if I was at the right place at the right time, then I would find the "right one." That is a common belief in many of my clients no matter what their vocation is or how much they have in their bank account. I have counseled and coached white collar to blue collar workers and the affluent to the indigent. It does not matter; they are still people. What I realize now after that light bulb moment is that we, at some point in our lives, alone feel emotional pain or suffering. Most of my clients initially seek treatment wondering *why* they stay stuck in the "what if" fear. I help them focus on the "what now." My what now was showing up for myself. Having a mindset of what now instead of *what if* meant that I let go of romanticizing and self-sabotaging and instead began giving myself *what* I want. I would still be the woman who pampers herself for hours, only this time the pampering was the expression of self-love and the elimination of self-hate.

I loved on myself by attending therapy weekly. I looked at myself proudly because I was being a freaking grown up and not a sad abandoned little girl who needed saving. In my sessions, I shared with my therapist all the grown-up things that I was doing. One session I shared with her how one guy contacted me two hours after we were supposed to meet. The little girl that used to show up to problems like that would accept whatever excuses a jerk like this would give. The adult me told him "This is a bad look for you. I don't do late" and never called him again. Powerful stuff for a woman who abandoned herself for most of her life. I explained to my therapist that this was pivotal for me because I feared being lonely so much in the past that I normally would have allowed such inconsideration. I would have even allowed him to go missing for a substantial about of time and accepted his call after not hearing from him. This type of self-abandonment would be my pursuit for a quick dopamine fix. I block this guy and I let go of an old tendency to feed addictive behavior because I am worth more than a quick high.

I was becoming an adult who was learning to own her self-worth, while letting go of showing up as an abandoned child who felt worthless. Building that self-worth meant embracing the value I already possessed, which led to making another adult decision--leaving my second husband (a second time). I acknowledged to myself that while my second husband and I are great friends, we were never meant to be partners. Staying in a marriage with a man whom I loved but was not in love with would be further self-abandonment. The fear of abandonment can be explained simply as the fear of being alone. Humans have a strong internal desire to be around other humans; they want to be a part of the herd. From a psychological standpoint, some humans unconsciously believe that when a relationship ends, it means they are unworthy of being with any one or being a part of the herd. One negatively perceived event in early childhood, particularly one that involves a caregiver or the absence of one, could lead to that individual developing that fear of being alone. The individual may develop the belief that they lack safety and are unworthy of care. I felt alone and negative about myself many nights as child. I would sit at the foot of my mother and stepfather's bedroom door in Indian style rocking back and forth, crying, and panicking afraid of being *alone* in my room. I would muffle my cries because I did not want to wake them up nor did I want the shame of them knowing my fear.

I feared many nights letting my husband go because it would bring up those panicky feelings. I hated feeling like a helpless child as a grown adult. Once I found the courage to release myself from this marriage, I allowed myself to sit with those panicky feelings, as they did arise, and noticed something. The feelings always passed. Sometimes the feelings were present longer than other times, but they always passed. I became better at allowing the feelings to *just be*. Soon I could sit with myself and enjoy myself. I started being more present with myself. I found things to enjoy in my present moment that before I'd overlooked worrying about being alone. I started enjoying living in my home more and laughing and joking with my children. I created things like crocheted blankets, new recipes, and redecorated my home. I started reaching out more to other humans where in the past I would avoid them due to fear of them not being around later. I took exotic and fun trips *alone* eating fine foods, staying in fancy places, drinking a few beers (before getting sober), and trying something new. Imagine taking yourself to Mexico, staying in a fancy hotel, going on an amazing day cruise snorkeling, and Latin dancing in the middle of the calle in Cancun. It was the best rendezvous I had ever had, and it was with myself—all by myself. Yet, I was not by myself. There were people everywhere. I just had to show up for myself to see it. I hope you are getting this. I resolved to be present for myself. Now, I was on the road to dating or accepting applications for a compatible partner ready to accept and embrace my present self-worth, capacity to show up for myself, and desire to be in a partner relationship.

Practical Healing Activity:

What is the best compliment you have ever given someone or wanted to give? What is the quality you are most fascinated with in other people? What is the deepest desire within you that you believe is impossible to accomplish or have? Take a moment close your eyes and see all the answers you gave. Now open your eyes and write down your answers. Each one of those things are possible if you commit to pursue them.

12. A Roadmap for Dating (Accept Applications)

I wish I knew of a good dating book or course prior to writing this book, especially since I had never "dated" per se. I have seen a few books that gave some guidance, but I needed the play-by-play steps on how to date. I didn't want to go at this dating thing fearfully-avoidant style. Thus, I took on the task of writing my own guide as I am sure I am not the only one who was ill equipped to date appropriately. I had been in serious relationships since the age of 14. I would meet someone and hang onto him. I realized later in life that all the people that I was in a relationship with were more like "friends with benefits" (FWB). Not the FWB that people are looking for on those cheesy dating apps. You know the ones where the guy or girl does not commit to a relationship but rather, they commitment to a "booty call" contract. The contract reads something like this "We are in each other's contacts. We call when we want to have sex. We probably will not hang out in public, and if we do, we do not identify as a couple. We do not identify as a couple. We are FWB." Derrick Jackson called this type of relationship a "situationship" in his book *Don't Forget Your Crown: Self-love Has Everything to Do with It*. Though I had some encounters like this, most of my relationships were with live-in partners, but we never dated prior to living together. If we enjoyed each other's company the first day or two, we became an item. We did not accept applications, interview each other, and we certainly did not take our time getting to know one another.

After two and half decades of FWB relationships, I decided to take a close look at myself and my pattern of showing up to relationships. I started dating, even though I initially hated it. Dating, in the beginning, was like going to the same interview over and over again. It was my pandemic Groundhogs Day. The cycle of pre-programmed dogma of what should be said or done manifested as boring phone conversations and text messages and dinners that seemed like a poker game. The senseless hiding annoyed me. He would try to hide his cards while I'd try to get to really know him--what he likes, his goals, fears, accomplishments, interests, and what makes him smile. I'd hear nonsense about how much he worked, how little time he had, and how he meets only women with drama. Listening to the nonsense and looking at him sideways like, "Asshole, I work and so does the rest of the planet. We all have the same 24 hours in a day. You are not that busy. Furthermore, if the women you have been dating have drama, then you are a key player in it."

After getting sober and having multiple dates like this, I realized I was attracting the same type of person—the asshole type. I also realized that women, myself included, come to the dating scene with bullshit, too. It all has to do social programming. The programming where women are expected to shy away from the conversation about sex, otherwise they will be perceived as "easy" or "a whore" or lose their perceived power by giving up the "candy" too soon. That programming is usually the woman's response to men evaluating them (or their perception of being evaluated) as being *too* sexual *too* soon or not being sexual enough. It is ridiculous. Both men and women need and want sex. They are mammals with primal needs like food, water, shelter, and sex. To what degree mammals need sex depends on the primate or human, but both genders need and want. Talking about sex for some humans seems to make people uncomfortable. For example, when two people encounter one another for the first time they may think to themselves *"Do we talk about sex on the first, second, or third date?" "Who should talk about it first?" "How much should we talk about it?" "Should we do it the first or second time we meet or wait 6 months or a year?"* It does not matter when or whether you have sex if you both consent to it. The only way you can consent is if you talk about sex openly and honestly. Dogs, which are also mammals, do not go around judging each other for thinking about sex, having sex too soon, or having too many past dog partners. Why should we? A dog seeks out another dog who has the same interest and they connect without judgment when they are both ready.

For some, being ready may relate to religious or moral values, and for others, it may be as simple as saying "yes." I'm not here to judge. What I am pointing out is that sex has become taboo in our society where discussing it is too far left or two far right instead of being wherever the heck the individuals chose. The thought of sex causes some people emotional distress even though it is a natural process. Many in society have been molded to believe sex is dirty—some due to past trauma and others from misinformation. Sex isn't dirty unless you want it to be (smile).

Our minds toward sex can be dirty if they are filled with shame and guilt instead of acceptance, pleasure, and peace. Let that soak in. I am not talking about the dirty mind where you spice up your bedroom playbook either. If we are honest, I think there's a little freak in all of us (as well it should be). I am talking about dirty as in viewing one's sexuality and sexual expression as dirty. We shame ourselves for seeking a basic need we all have. Accepting sex as a basic human need, like having food and water, and meeting that need in a healthy way is normal. That's right, if you consent to have sex with another consenting adult—IT. IS. NORMAL. Embrace yourself as a sexual being and your need to express your sexuality. (*I want to be clear that I am talking about consensual sex. Minors or individuals who have been deemed by a court as incapacitated are not able to give consent*). To find the right man or woman for you, you must be willing to openly communicate all aspects of yourself including your feelings and desires about sex, past sexual experiences, your sexuality, and your sexual needs. Not talking about these issues openly results in sexual frustration, affairs, and emotional distress.

While healthy sexual expression in a relationship is vital, similar core values are just as imperative. Core values relate to the basic moral compass that drives us. During the dating or interviewing and application phase, individuals should be asking and assessing whether their potential partner has similar core values. There are numerous core values such as acceptance, love, discipline, honesty, respect, trustworthiness, loyalty, security, and responsibility. One of the main core values that I look for in a partner is acceptance, as this is a value that drives me that I denied for years. Acceptance means being open and accepting of one's self and others as they are in that moment. It means not interacting or refusing to interact with someone based on a past or perceived version of him or even myself. Acceptance further means actively choosing whether to be in relationship with someone instead of mindlessly entering into one. Acceptance is the act of allowing one's self and others to express their free will and unique qualities.

With my new commitment to embrace self-acceptance, I choose whether I align myself with anyone romantically, personally, or professionally. Dating is the stage where you need to pay close attention to the other person's professed and manifested core values before determining whether to commit to a relationship with him or her. A professed core value is what one says, but a manifested core value is what one does. You may meet someone, for instance, who professes to be open-minded. Yet, you notice that each time you share something with this person that differs from his worldview he finds a way to change or dismiss it. The person in this case likely is not open-minded.

Likewise, some other examples of behaviors that demonstrate a lack of openness are changing the subject, dominating most conversations with his opinions, providing constant "evidence" that your viewpoint is invalid, bringing other people into the conversation to sway your view and validate his own, being intolerant of talking about what matters to you, or lacking tolerance of your right to be and think differently. Aligning with someone who is intolerant of your core values or whose moral compass and intrinsic values differ greatly from your own spells d-i-s-a-s-t-e-r. Disaster leads to unhappiness. No one wants to be unhappy.

Before you start accepting applications, you need to be clear on what happiness is. The U.S. Constitution says Americans are entitled to "life, liberty, and the pursuit of happiness." The pursuit of happiness is where most people get stuck. The gauge for that pursuit, for many, is based on social programming, social media, the opinions of family and friends, religion, or other prescribed precept. Pursuing happiness based on all those components means that one's happiness is fluid, intangible, and unrealistic. This type of pursuit is about a destination that individuals try to reach from others' viewpoint instead of living a life defining one's own concept of happiness.

The person that lacks self-awareness in this area consciously competing against others, but the real competition is against his own unconscious desire to not compete all. The person's real desire is to *just be* who they are. That is happiness. Imagine trying to live a life like the Kardashians or Will and Jada Smith. That forfeits the beautiful expression of your uniquely designed light—you a beacon (inspiration) remember. To pursue something means to chase after it. Chase the happiness that lies within. If anything about Will and Jada's story inspires you, let it be that after 25 years of publicizing a perfect marriage, they revealed that they were deeply unhappy living the *perfect* lie. Happiness is not about being perfect. Chasing the happiness within means you have to resist the urge to be phony and embrace the challenges that life brings to be *just you.* Rather than looking for the perfect version of yourself and the perfect version of someone else, embrace a new idea. Two people willing to openly express their true being and accept their perceived imperfections can foster true happiness in both.

A Roadmap for Dating

Dating myself, I learned to show up to dates with men prepared to walk away from the encounter at any time if there is no alignment. This is Rule I—*Dating is the trial period; it is not the purchasing phase.* The rule applies to dating yourself or someone else. If you explore something new, you give it a trial period to determine if you want to make that a part of who you are. Likewise, dating someone is interacting with him to what degree you feel comfortable to see if he or she is who you want and willing to accept as they are in that moment. *Am I attracted to him physically? Does he possess the moral character that I seek? Can I see myself spending 5 minutes, 5 years, or 50 years with him? Is he a free thinker or someone who needs caretaking?* My previous decades of relationships I approached dating like purchasing a car without testing driving it. I always showed up ready "to get married, live in a house with the white picket fence, and have kids" dream. The healthier version of myself showed up to each date with the mentality that I am on a date with myself and I am allowing my date to access me so I can determine if I want to be in an ongoing relationship with him. By date, I don't just mean dinner or a movie, I am my entire initial experience with that person before I ever decide to give him status in my life. Far too often, we give people status in our life that we have not vetted or qualified as status worthy. We call people "friend" whom we just met. We say "this is my lady" or "this is my man" after going on a few night outs on the town. Instead of just giving status, we need to pre-qualify the person.

I have four other rules pre-qualification rules for dating. I use the acronym R.O.A.D. to help me remember these four relationship mapping principles. I share these with my clients who seek my help while they are dating. A potential suitor must meet these requirements to maintain access in my physical and emotional space. This ROADmap I created is a filtering process that allows me to focus on the person who **is** in front of me as opposed to focusing on what I **hope** he will become.

    R = Recognize Red Flags
    O = Observe and Listen
    A = Assess Wisely
    D = Decide on the Dealbreakers

Recognize Red Flags

Trauma survivors who have not learned healthy life habits usually overlook red flags in potential partners because they are driven by feelings of inadequacy (lack of self-worth). Recognize the 'R' in the ROADmap or red flags. Red flags are toxic (dangerous or destructive) qualities or behaviors a potential person displays that you should avoid at all cost (with the highest cost being your emotional and physical safety. Remember red means DANGER! If you are a trauma survivor, think about your last (or current) relationship. How many of the things did your partner do that hurt you that you saw in the beginning but ignored because he was "a nice guy" or she was a "really sweet girl?" How many things about that partner went unnoticed until you were emotionally entrenched in the relationship? I have dated enough toxic people I could probably write another chapter or book just on red flags.

Red flags are things that some people overlook who suffer from past trauma because they are developmentally accustomed to accepting them. They may have seen their parents or caregivers abuse one another or been abused by them. They may have experienced sexual or physical trauma in childhood, as I did, at a young age. They may have been assaulted by a stranger in their past. Their trauma may have resulted in repressed memories about the trauma or traumas. Adapting to the effects of trauma, they may have taught themselves to avoid conflict, not advocate for themselves, believe that certain behavior is acceptable and healthy, or learn to trust people way too soon.

These maladaptive beliefs and patterns of relating to a partner or others likely demonstrate the persons inability to set and maintain boundaries with themselves or other people.

Boundaries are concept that people have either never heard of or vaguely understand. A boundary is an emotional and physical property line that outlines where you begin and end. It is a line that differentiates you from another. Think about your home and the property that it sits on. Imagine for a moment the home and property next to yours. Now, think about the home on the other side of your home. *How do you know where your property line begins and ends?* For most homeowners, a surveyor has surveyed the property and provided written indication of where the owner's property lines, or boundaries are. That indication shows where those boundaries are in relation to the two adjacent homes. Some homeowners choose to place a fence around their home to represent or reinforce where those property lines are. Similarly, anyone interacting with another person must clearly and succinctly express and reinforce his boundaries. The owner's fence shows neighbors and bystanders a clear indication that the area inside the fence is someone's property and requires permission for access. Further, the door, windows, and framed structure of the home, shows them that the inside requires additional permission for access. Likewise, communicating with someone about what conditions enables them access to your emotional and physical space is a healthy conflict resolution skill.

A boundary is clear point of reference that must be set to address when a property line has been crossed, that is, when resolving a conflict. Some people do not understand how to set boundaries to create emotional and physical protection. Once a person understands what a boundary is, then they must learn to set and maintain it. To set a boundary, one must identify who owns the property. Emotional and relational property can be feelings, attitudes, behaviors, and problems to name a few. If you have a feeling or an attitude about something, you own it. If you behave a certain way, you own that behavior. If there is a problem that needs fixing, gain awareness of who owns the problem (whose fence it is in) before you think about solving it. The one who has the feeling, attitude, behavior, or problem, owns it. If it is not your feelings, it is not your problem. Almost every therapy and coaching session, a client says, "I don't want to hurt their feelings" or "I don't want people to be mad with me." I realize as soon the client says this, he or she does not understand enough about boundaries and likely have few healthy boundaries with themselves or others. I am aware of this because their language indicates a belief that they own or control the other person's feelings.

Feelings represent the meaning an individual places on an experience his or her experience. No one interprets that experience for them. Trauma survivors often have heard from their abusers that they "made" something happen, which often results in them developing the belief that they have magical powers to create other people's feelings. The fact is they cannot *hurt* anyone's feelings or make someone *mad* because they do not own their feelings.

Here is a scenario to consider. Ten people go to see a movie. After the movie, seven people say, "That movie sucked; I can't believe I wasted my money on it." The other three people say, "That movie rocked; let's go see it again." Who is right and who is wrong? No one. It is how they interpreted the movie based on their life experiences (good, bad, or indifferent) and their current mood. They own the interpretations or the feelings they have about their experience. When interacting with someone, remember Rule 2— *You are only responsible for and can change what you own.*

Rule 2 is about identifying what the problem is and where the problem is. Are another person's feelings the problem? Then, it is outside of your property line. You do not own it. It is not your responsibility. Allow them to resolve or address their property, that is, their feelings. If there is a problem, you should not automatically try to solve it unless you have identified that it is in your property line. Trauma survivors--notice I didn't say victims--must learn to develop and apply this concept of ownership in their relationships. They will become masters of their own personal safety by adapting this skill in their daily lives and ultimately building an environment to protect and save themselves from predators. Each individual owns his or her own their limits, desires, thoughts, values, choices, talents, and love as Drs. Henry Cloud and John Townsend shared in their book called *Boundaries*. Remember that and only take responsibility for what you own.

Here's questions you can ask yourself while dating about ownership:

- Who is responsible for my time?

- When do I receive calls or respond to text messages?
- How do I feel about my interaction with this person?
- Does my date respect my time, availability, feelings, and other areas I own to which I have given him access?

What is important for you to understand is boundaries give you freedom. You need to develop the self-awareness of what you own and what you are responsible and determine what does not belong to you. Once you make this decision, you have the freedom of choice. I get it having a history of an abuse can make you believe that you no longer have control because someone forced their control on you in the past. Your abuse is in your past. Each interaction that happens in the present is happening now. Your past does not define you. Your boundaries in the present moment do. Boundaries protect you from a toxic relationship or a controlling encounter. You decide who, what, when, where, and how long someone has access to you. Deciding who has access has these benefits:

- Allow a potential partner and others to address their own well-being as competent adults to decide who they allow access in their property lines instead of you.
- Create your protection from toxic behavior and people, excessive fear, and excessive pain.
- Increase your self-worth, self-respect, and self-acceptance by only accepting and protecting what you own.
- Gain the respect of others because you set and maintain your accessibility which promotes a healthy living environment.
- Develop your ability to be assertive in speech and behavior about your boundaries rather than expecting people to just figure it out.

Regarding a healthy living environment, you must develop an understanding of toxic or problematic behaviors that warrant setting and maintaining boundaries. I created a long, though not exhaustive, list of behaviors I have encountered in my relationship journey and those clients have reported to me over the years.

- Communicates in a condescending (talking down) manner

- Overly critical or judgmental
- Gaslighting or using psychological games to make someone question if he or she is "crazy" or insane.
- Guilt tripping or making someone feel "bad" or "low" for not doing or saying something
- Ignoring you
- Only texting, never calling
- Financial abuse such as using money or lack thereof to control someone's behavior
- Cyber or digital bullying (e.g., saying mean things on social media about someone)
- Isolating you from others (e.g., keeping someone from seeing their family or friends)
- Devaluing you or your accomplishments
- Intimidating (e.g., overtalking someone, using one's physical presence or an aggressive tone to make someone do something)
- Parenting you (e.g., interacting with someone like he or she is a child rather than interacting with him or her like he or she is capable of making decisions and solving his or her own problems)

- Neglecting (e.g., not being attentive during conversations, showing up late for dates or planned activities)
- Becoming easily irritated or upset, which demonstrates lack of self-control and emotional dysregulation
- Destroying property
- Stalking (e.g., conveniently showing up where you are, mysterious phone calls or messages or hang ups, knowing information about you before you give it)

I have seen these behaviors anywhere from the first to the third encounter in past toxic relationships. They were not subtle at all. I just ignored them confusing these behaviors with love and giving me attention. I would confront some of these behaviors and be given a poor excuse for them. For example, with the increase of many people being online, I began online dating again. Most people were not interested in communicating in person only texting. They would give a lame excuse about how busy they were to talk yet have no problem texting me for hours. Another example was a date who did not show up when he said he would. He gaslighted me for confronting him saying, "I don't remember saying that. That's not what I said." Guilt tripping is yet another example where a date devalued me because I said something that differed from his opinion saying something like, "I was trying to see you, but it seems like you're not in the mood." With this in mind, here are a few more toxic behaviors that you may display that attracts an unhealthy person to you or that they may display own their own.

- Telling it all the first few dates.
- Talking intimately the first time you meet someone. (e.g., "I love you," "I just can't wait to see you again.")
- Falling in love with a new acquaintance.
- Being overwhelmed by a person.
- Not noticing when someone else has inappropriate boundaries.
- Accepting gifts or touches that you do not want.
- Taking too much in order "to be nice."
- Giving too much in order "to be nice."
- Letting others tell you what to do and when to do it.
- Letting others tell you how you feel or invalidate your feelings.
- Thinking others can read your mind.
- Expecting others to set or maintain boundaries for you.
- Overeating.
- Not getting adequate sleep.
- Mismanaging money or overspending.

- Talking bad about other people or gossiping.
- Self-abuse such as addiction, being a martyr for other people, or inflicting physical or emotional harm

(Important: If you live in the United States and feel you are in danger of hurting yourself or someone else, please call 911 or emergency services in your area, or visit your local emergency room. You can also reach out to the crisis line any time if you need to talk to someone when you feel overwhelmed or not sure if you want to hurt yourself at 1-800-273-TALK (8255) or through chat at 741741. If you believe you may be experiencing domestic violence, you can contact 1-800-799-SAFE (7233) or through chat at 741741. You are never alone. If you are in danger or hurting yourself or are in a domestic violence situation and you live outside the United States, please contact your local emergency services for assistance.)

Observe

Red flags can either be obvious or go unnoticed. It is your responsibility to take an active part in devising healthy confrontation through observation. Observation, 'O' in ROADmap, is necessary and can be accomplished by asking questions and listening for the answers. Taking someone to dinner or out on the town is an easy task for most to accomplish, especially a manipulator or a toxic person. It is more challenging; however, for a toxic person to hide the way he or she handles conflict with others or more importantly with you. Observe how your date interacts during a conflict with the store clerk, wait staff, his family, and friends. These are clear indicators of how he or she will interact with you.

- *Does he avoid conflict it?*
- *Does he get upset easily?*
- *Is he rude?*
- *Does he habitually blame others and ignore his role in the conflict?*
- *Does he play the victim?*
- *Does he hold grudges toward a person after saying a conflict is resolved?*
- *Does he seek out others to vent about the conflict and fail to discuss with the person(s) involved?*

In addition to observing how your date handles conflict, observe how he handles his money, cares for his home, takes care of his children, addresses his hygiene, communicates with or about his ex, views working, and discusses his future. Consider if the way he or she handles these things align with your beliefs and needs. If he is an overspender and you are a saver, will his spending habits impact your ability to save and result in financial distress down the road for you and the relationship? If he rarely sees his children, will he be a healthy, active partner for your children if the two of you decide to have children or to your children if you already have children? Observation takes time and should not be thought of as going through the express or self-checkout in Walmart to purchase a few snacks and household items. Observation should be thought of more like looking at an expensive home to decide whether you want to pay the asking price to purchase it. You want to check out the electrical, mechanical, heating, structure, and space to ensure that it adequate for you to inhabit You would not want to spend a million dollars on home only to find out that it looked pretty at first glance, but it won't hold up any better than the home on the old movie *The Money Pit*. Likewise, you do not want to quickly glance at your date only observing surface qualities such as he's handsome, has a nice, looks like he works, and seems self-reliant. Later discovering, he doesn't shower, eats unhealthily, doesn't exercise, talks crappy to you, can't hold a job or save a dime, and expects you to provide for him financially and emotionally. I've been down that road before and trust me; it's not a good look. The relationship is unfulfilling and leads to more trauma. Observe this person well to determine the behaviors and values the person demonstrates consistently, then decision whether what you have seen aligns with you. During the observation phase, you gather adequate information to determine whether it is safe to give the person access into your life. In other words, can you trust him or her?

Assess Wisely

Trust is earned not given; for that reason, trust--do not rush--the process. Up to this point in the dating phase, optimistically, you have determined whether there are any red flags ("stranger danger"). You have observed and listened intently for answers to the trust question. Now is the time to use wisdom and discernment to assess the data you have received from your encounters with this person and cross reference them with guide. You have not committed to anything but review this person's application. Reviewing it requires you to assess wisely all you have seen and heard and deciding whether further interaction, conflict, or additional questions are warranted or even desired. This step in the process requires razor sharp focus on what is and not on what you hope it might be. Avoid the love money pit by doing your due diligence—do not skip the 'A' in ROADmap.

Decide on the Dealbreakers

The 'D' in ROADmap is my favorite step in the process. It is the part where I believe an individual has the most power in relating to other humans. You decide if there is a *deal or no deal*. YOU. No one else. You. No one can force you to be in relationship with them. He isn't the only sailor on the ship. She isn't the only fish in the sea. You did not waste your time. You stuck to the process. Dating is a process. I had a ton of patience with myself through 2020 as I dated myself. Even when I wanted to be impatient, I refused because there was no rush in getting to know and accept myself. I did not allow any one I dated or interacted with to get impatient or rush me either. I respected their right to choose whether I had access to their property. In some cases, my being patient with myself was something that did not align with some suitors. That was okay by me. One guy after became frustrated because I did not consent to sex after a few dates. He felt that since he was ready, I should be too. I wasn't. My response to his impatience, "You may want to find someone who moves faster than me." He agreed. We did not talk after that. It felt good. I used my power and decided who has access to me and when, not someone else. I set and maintain the boundary to maintain my physical and emotional safety. Someone professing to want a committed relationship who needs me to decide *right now* on sex or anything for that matter demonstrates qualities such as intolerance, dominance, and poor awareness. These qualities are dealbreakers--the *road*, dating road that is, stops here.

Dealbreakers clarify what you really want. Before I just wanted somebody to be around me all the time to avoid the fear of abandonment and maintain that addict's high. Once I let go self-hate and self-abandonment and embraced self-acceptance, my perspective changed, and I identified just the type of partner I wanted in my life. I realized I did not want a space holder, I wanted someone to hold space. I wanted someone who would show up. I wanted someone with good moral character and drive. I wanted someone built to take on the world. I wanted someone like me. *Imagine that!* Someone who aligns with you is compatible with you. If he is not compatible, that is the dealbreaker. No matter how you feel, what other people think about him, how lonely you are, or what he has or drives, if he is not compatible, REJECT. THE. APPLICATION. Relationships cannot be built on potential qualities. Here is a bullet point of my dealbreakers to give you an idea for creating your own.

- Present
- Handsome
- Open and honest communicator
- Chivalric
- Dependable (show up on time, impeccable with his word)
- Masculine energy and comfortable in it
- Leader with compassion
- Lover of all things dance (I cannot emphasize this enough)
- Outgoing (I hate a homebody)
- Adventurous (I don't do boring)
- Accepting of self and others
- Committed to healthy conflict resolution
- Intellectual conversation (uses knowledge and intellect with wisdom)
- Pragmatic
- Traveler

- Wild animal in bed or car or bathroom or wherever (a must)
- Funny (corny acceptable)
- Family-oriented
- Goal-oriented
- Driven by purpose
- Fit
- Fun
- Exciting
- Rejects the status quo
- God-fearing (agnostic and atheists automatically disqualified)

These characteristics are important to me along with basic core values such as good moral character, acceptance, and commitment. For instance, with all the things I shared in this book, there are some who may not accept me because of who I am and what I have experienced. That is okay (Learn to say that when things are just the way that they are— *That is okay*). What I am not okay with is partnering with a man who cannot accept that I have a past, I can be moody at times, I love to be on the go, I am a recovering addict, my sexuality isn't "normal," and I'm a hell of a lot of fun. Accepting that at times, I may have a sexual attraction to a woman without the desire or intent to be in relationship with her may be a hard thing for a man to do. Embracing someone who is fully accepting of her sexuality, without having to label her sexuality the way society does, may be too much for a man who has not embraced his own sexuality. Likewise, a man unable to embrace his masculinity could never support me fully in embracing my femininity. My list may not match other people's, but it must match or be compatible with the next man I align myself. I have zero interest in someone who may potentially develop these traits. He must come to the table with them or he does not eat at my table. *I love this self-worth stuff.*

As a final note in this chapter, I want to share with you the letter I wrote to my future partner in life. It outlines the vision I have for us and how we would align. You should be just as clear about who you want to move from dating to partner as I am, and I am committed to it.

A Letter to My King

Dear Mi Rey,

I must write to you as the matters of my heart are heavy. There is much for a king to do and caring for your queen is a priority, cariño. An hombre of your caliber can handle me I am sure as long as I tell you everything. You don't have to approach me in wonder or uncertainty because you are whom I seek.

Allow me to confirm this for you as I describe my sentiments to the detail.

You are a Believer in God as your Creator and Sustainer. You understand that by the hands of God it is possible for us to share this small space in time.

Your words are not full of flattery, but they are full of the spice of honesty. I trust them wholeheartedly.

Your eyes that pierce my soul have you preserved to adorn me solely. I dress my cuerpo in garments that catch your attention, but the attire of my heart is what captivates you.

Your vulnerability takes healthy risks to connect and build intimacy with me as you are not too afraid to expose your true inner being. My fire stays lit because of it.

Your integrity, the part of you that lines up with the part of you that no one sees, is noteworthy and puts smooth criminals to shame.

You keep your word consistently displaying results instead of ruckus. You are as dependable as a canine.

Your drive and pursuit of dream-life goals is why I represent the kingdom while you battle the world daily. Know my fierce lion, no one will penetrate our kingdom as I will guard it with my own sword and shield. It is my pleasure to die for the bond we have built.

Your commitment is like the beaver that demonstrates the willingness, dedication, and skill to get the job done in our business and for our family.

You hunt and kill meat for our table but also seek after your queen for pleasure and rest. I will ensure I prepare your table and bed with all the pleasantries you deserve, my wild lion.

You protect and defend our kingdom, including your queen's crown, at all cost including your pride. I am proud to call you "Your Highness."

You freely boast your position as king and my position next to your beautiful throne.

Your humor makes me laugh often as we chat about the wonders of this life.

You excite us with adventure and allow me to excite us with the same. I cherish our play dates.

You understand that love is an action that must be repeated daily. I, too, have embraced this which is why I send this letter of love. *Te amo mucho, chulito.*

You're tall and attractive with a nice build. I admire the way you care for your body so that we can enjoy each other on this rock as long as possible.

You are secure in yourself to include your insecurities. You refuse to project your insecurities onto others or me. Instead, you share your insecurities with me as we pillow talk the night away making our kingdom fortified.

You generally are happy in life and actively take steps to promote healthy gratification. I follow your lead, mi ángel.

The champions gravitate to you because you are a battle ax in times of war.

You admonish the healthy qualities in your queen and nurture her in her imperfect humanness.

You are my best friend, whom I trust and run to when the world gets heavy.

You are a King fit for a dozen kingdoms, an empire even. But you chose decisively our kingdom, where you converse with your queen, mi corazón, in secret to decide and accomplish plans together. You don't dictate mi vida, but you entrap mi alma.

The day will come when we embrace. Until then, I await you, mi amor.

Stay strong para mi,

Your Queen"

(Facebook post on December 1, 2019)

Practical Healing Activity:

Create your own dealbreaker list or letter. Remember having this list at the forefront of your mind gives you the power to create and maintain your own physical and emotional safety and decide who has access to you.

13. Build and Grow a Healthy Relationship (Commit)

I only want royalty *eating at my table*--the king. I do not allow people to enter my home or break bread at my sacred table unless I am in relationship with them. Growing up, my mother, who is a missionary, welcomed many people into our home. During her 17 years working in civil service, she invited service members who were away from their families to our home during the holidays. I always enjoyed these festivities and meeting new people. She also allowed extended family members to live with us to help them get on their feet over the years. I honored this hospitable quality in my mother.

As I young adult, I tried to emulate her hospitality by inviting coworkers and friends into my home. I cooked big meals, played music, and served alcohol. When I bought my first home, I was so excited about this accomplishment, I wanted to share it with others. I remember an older lady that worked with me inviting herself to my home as if she were celebrating with me. She quickly befriended me. She visited my home, we hung out, and she traveled out of town with me once to a hair show when I was a cosmetologist. It was not until after all these things we shared that I noticed her character. She gossiped at work about other people, tattled on coworkers to our supervisor. She was only nice on the surface. My lack of observation of her poor moral character was problematic for me. Coworkers soon began to enlighten me about her toxicity indicating she frequently talked about me behind my back. They said she called my home small, talked bad about my husband and children, and said unkind things about me. My interaction and lack of proper observation of this woman taught me that everyone is not qualified to eat at my table. My mother likely knew this, but I had to learn it the hard way.

My mother possessed something I had not developed at that time, something called emotional intelligence—which is not the same thing as the ability to learn concrete information. Emotional intelligence is the capacity to recognize, know, use, and manage one's emotions in a healthy way to reduce or eliminate stress, communicate well, be empathic toward others, and rise above internal and external conflict. I had believed my cognitive intelligence or smarts was all I needed to relate to people. I recall my mother telling me time and time again growing up, "You've got book smarts, but you ain't got no common sense." She essentially was telling me I lacked emotional intelligence. Being book smart relates to having facts and knowledge, but emotional intelligence is about understanding relationship.

- *How does one view and relates to him or herself and others?*
- *How effectively does one resolve his or her own emotions or feelings about a situation?*
- *Can the person communicate those feelings effectively and independently?*
- *How does one connect or interact with others in an intentional way that supports what is important to him or her?*
- *Does one make informed decisions or emotional ones in terms of relationships?*

These are important perspectives to understand when developing a relationship with one's self and others. The unhealthy relationships and situationships I had through the years were because I was an emotional hot mess. My emotional dysregulation was the direct result of my past trauma and poor guidance on how to respond appropriately to my emotions or and then create the necessary boundaries to resolve the conflict adequately.

Having the emotional self-control enables me to grow in relationship with someone else. Emotions are not a problem. You are an emotional being. It is how we respond to those emotions that can be problematic. I am growing in my dating relationship because I am fostering a healthy emotional relationship with myself. I no longer allow myself to be too clingy or too distant when I am trying to get to know someone. I moved about 45 minutes away from my hometown and family a month before I started the dating relationship. For me, it was like moving into the middle of nowhere. Many businesses and social places were closed because of the coronavirus pandemic—that in my opinion was prolonged due to political corruption, the presidential election, and it being a census year. I had ended two long-term friendships, and I typically was alone as my son only stayed with me part-time. (Though, I did have my beagle-hound, Peanut, around).

Consider someone who fears abandonment moving from her home in a familiar town to a sizeable apartment in a strange one--alone. I would have intense moments where I felt lonely, depressed, and worthless because of the grief of starting over, living by myself, and once again not being in a relationship with someone who offered healthy companionship. Before I reached the emotional place, I am in now, I might have grabbed a beer or called an old lover to cope with those feelings. Since I was dating, I could have called a person of interest who I had gone on a few dates with. Instead, however, I did what an emotionally intelligent person would do: I resolved the feelings independently and built a deeper relationship with myself. I only called the person after I knew I was calling him for companionship and not for rescue, which meant when he showed up, I was dating him and not using him as an object of safety. Relationships can be wonderful experiences, even if they do not last forever, if people showed up to relationships having emotionally resolved their own problems and deciding to relate to another person only after reaching that resolution.

I created a technique for my clients to resolve emotional dysregulation (or self-regulate) and use emotional intelligence in their lives based on cognitive-behavioral therapy. The technique is called "Check Your ETA." Your ETA stands for your emotions, thoughts, and actions. (If you haven't already noticed, I love to create plays on words and use mnemonic references, as it helps people to remember them). In the same way you learned your ABCs through the ABC song in preschool, you can learn to develop new habits through self-awareness and memorization. ETA has to do with arrival. *What's your ETA?* We've heard it so many times. Now, you have a *new* ETA. It is your emotions—your thoughts about those emotions—and your reactions (or responses to those former two). The goal of checking your ETA is to be emotionally and physically responsive, not reactive.

Ask yourself, "What do I feel?" Survivors of trauma or those who lack emotional intelligence have a difficult time answering this question. In therapy sessions with trauma survivors, I have heard responses such as "I don't know," "sadness," "anger," or "nothing." I have had similar responses from those who have been married for decades. As a culture we have not been taught to identify our emotions. We have been programmed to just be emotional. There is a difference. Identifying your emotions or feelings means recognizing chemical reactions that are presented somewhere in your body signaling that something needs to be addressed. Thirst, for example, is a feeling or signal (**emotion**) that is often felt in the stomach, yet it is sometimes mistaken for hunger by the brain.

Many people interpret "I am hungry" (**thought**) as a feeling and then react (re-**action**) to it by eating a meal or hefty snack. Later, they realize they have overeaten, as they may have eaten recently. Ideally, you should experience the *emotion* by sitting with it, thinking about it, processing the signal, and then responding to the emotion or signal.

Here is an actual scenario of me using ETA. I was stuck in traffic inching through tunnel after work headed home to meet my partner at the time so we could go to dinner. I felt angry, impatient, anxious, fearful, helpless, and worn out. I thought about the anger, traffic, dinner, and my other feelings. My legs were shaking. I cracked my knuckles. I cursed at other drivers through the window. My breathing was shallow. I dipped in and out of traffic. I felt nauseous.

ETA Rule I: *Recognize the context by stating what, where, when, and who else is involved.*

- What – I was stuck in traffic
- Where – In the tunnel
- When – After work
- Who else was involved – My partner

*ETA Rule 2: Identify your **emotions**.*

- Angry
- Impatient
- Anxious
- Fearful
- Helpless
- Worn out
- Nauseous

*ETA Rule 3: Say out loud (or write down) your **thoughts**.*

- I feel angry because I hate traffic.
- Why is there traffic now?
- I want to get home to see my partner now.
- I am afraid he will get upset if I am late and won't want to go out.
- I can't do anything but sit here.
- I've been working all day long.
- I'm going to be sick.

ETA Rule 4: Examine whether your behaviors are a reaction or response. (**actions**).

- Shaking legs
- Cracking knuckles
- Cursing at the window
- Shallow breathing
- Dipping in and out traffic
- Making myself sick

ETA Rule 5: Stop to think of what you really want to happen (**new thought**).

- I want to go to dinner with my partner and have time to change my clothes so I will look nice for him.

ETA Rule 6: Recognize why what you want is important to you (**identify new feelings**).

- I miss spending quality time with my partner as we haven't been out in a few weeks.
- I want to wear something he likes and feel sexy in it.
- I'm hungry and want to eat good food.

ETA Rule 7: Decide what you are willing to do to make what is important to you happen (**plan new actions**).

- I will listen to music that will distract me from my negative thoughts and relax me while I wait in traffic.
- I will call my partner and tell him I am stuck in traffic and let him know that I need extra time to get ready when I arrive.

ETA Rule 8: Determine what, if anything about this situation, will matter 5 minutes or 5 years from now (**reinforcing new thoughts**).

- Traffic won't matter after I call my partner to tell him I'm stuck in it.
- Spending time with my partner will matter 5 minutes from now.
- I'm not sure if spending time with my partner will matter 5 years from now.
- Overacting, instead of responding, likely will matter 5 minutes from now as I may be too anxious, irritable,

and nauseous when I see my partner and not enjoy myself at dinner.

ETA Rule 9: *Commit and Act*

- Exercise your emotional intelligence by acting on what you outlined at Rule 7 and give yourself a pep talk with what you realized at Rule 9.
- Celebrate working and committing to the steps.

ETA Rule 10: *Repeat. Repeat. Repeat.*

- Do all of these steps in the same order until you have resolved the conflict with yourself or others in an emotionally intelligent way.

Those steps will help you to take the guesswork out of conflict resolution in relationship—building or maintaining them. This entire book is about learning to know and trust yourself. It is a guide. If you are a trauma survivor or you like instant gratification, I encourage you to let go of the need to be pleased in the moment. You will never fully develop emotional maturity until you do. I broke down each step so that you can evaluate at any time when you are listening to and being true with yourself. You can determine if the problem is with you or someone else. If you are not doing the steps, you will get caught up blaming other people, harboring unforgiveness, feeling worthless, and falling back into that trap of self-abandonment. You're better than that! Trust the process. Date you. Correct you. Then, address other people accordingly.

Practical Healing Activity:

Use the technique "Check Your ETA" to address a current conflict you are facing. My definition of "current" is within the last week. Anything longer than that and you run the risk of poor self-evaluation because most humans do not remember as well as they think they do. Trauma survivors, in particular, tend to struggle with memory or distorted thinking. It is best for the conflict to be something that is fresh on your mind, but it does not have to be a huge deal. I prefer that the conflict to be something you are avoiding, someone you are avoiding talking to, or whatever came to your mind when I told you to do this exercise. Do that now. Do not forget that relaxing sounds and a quiet space help to create an atmosphere where you can hear *you* and not a ton of distractions.

14. Never Stop Dating You (Be Unmasked)

Life can be a distraction. If you allow it, life challenges can lead you away from the useful advice I shared with you in this book. Self-acceptance is not a box you check on a form; it is a way of being. You are a be-*ing*. The -ing signifies an ongoing action. You are always *being* something, but who that is depends on you. By never stopping dating yourself, you can develop emotional intelligence about who you are in relation to those around you.

Always consider how you experience yourself.

1. *Do you view yourself as a beacon of light and worth, and if so, are you **being** that worthy light?*

2. *Do you find yourself at times shining brighter than at other times, and if so, are you wearing a mask when light is dim?*

3. *If you are wearing a mask, are you willing to continue to abandon yourself in that way, or are you willing to*

commit to checking your ETA to align or re-align them with who you are?

4. *Are you showing up to a potential suitor or friendship recognizing that you control their access to you, or are you leaving the door open to further trauma, guilt, and grief?*

5. *Have you let go of perceived past injustices, choosing to forgive, and rejecting the need for closure, or are you waiting for the past to be undone so you can start living in the present?*

6. *Are you accepting of your sexuality, label, or whatever you call it and expressing it how you see fit, or are you attempting to fit yourself into societal "norms" about sexuality?*

7. *Have you committed to build and grow in a relationship with yourself before relating to anyone else?*

8. *Have you embraced, after hearing self-hating stories I once told myself, that you and only you choose to live UNMASKED?*

Love,

Dr. D

Follow with Dr. D

Facebook, Instagram, Twitter, Pinterest, Parler, LinkedIn, and Tik Tok

@followdrdeee

Subscribe and like my YouTube channel:

https://www.youtube.com/channel/UCRC2NsAw5yetnj99YjaxEUA

Visit my website:

www.azzerturself.com

Acknowledgements

I would like to thank my daughter, Ascha, who set the example for me to embrace the other parts of me I tried to deny. As I told you sweetie, you showed mami courage I wish I had at a younger age. I've always said we grew up together and honestly sometimes you grew a little quicker than me. I am **SUPER** proud of you.

I would like to thank my oldest friend, David, who stood by my side watching and supporting the journey unfolding for more than 25 years and counting. The many tearful nights you listened without judgment as I worked hard to figure the ties that bound me. You never looked at me any less than the beautiful woman that I am, expressing your unconditional, accepting love long before I ever embraced my own self-acceptance. I love you.

About the Author

Dr. Danita Morales Ramos is a clinical psychologist known to her followers and clients as "Dr. D," founded her private practice Azz-ert Urself! LLC Mindset Coaching and Counseling in 2018. She expanded her business globally through virtual and in-person mindset coaching and therapy and through social media. She holds a Doctor of Philosophy degree in Clinical Psychology from Walden University, is licensed in multiple states through the United States, and is the published author of **_From the Voice of a Fractured Mind:_**

Speak Loud and *Finding Your Voice: A Guided Journal to Mental Clarity*.

Dating Yourself Unmasked: A Guiding Light from Sexual Trauma to Self-Acceptance is the published work she gifted to herself as a Christmas present. Dr. D not only is an expert in overcoming self-concealment, but she is also a connoisseur of the very strategies she develops and teaches her clients. It is through her ever-evolving personal therapeutic journey that she perfects her craft of helping others to live their best quality of life assertively. She can discover more about Dr. D and the service she offers, to include coaching groups, and webinars, and public speaking at her website (https://azzerturself.com/).

Made in United States
Orlando, FL
19 May 2022